"In *Send*, Jim issues a compell:
ture a sending culture, cham
clarity and biblical fidelity, Ji. _____ course for churches to
multiply locally through strategic church planting and local missions, while simultaneously reaching out globally through dynamic engagement in frontier missions. This is a book that will stir your soul, enlarge your perspective, and spur you to joyful obedience as we labor together for the day when God's glory covers the earth as the waters cover the seas."

MATT CARTER, VP of Mobilization, Send Network,
North American Mission Board

"Jim Essian has served the church beautifully well in writing this short book that packs a huge punch. Founded upon the character of our sending God and his vision for his world, Jim calls us, simply, to join with our God in his sovereign plans. This would be a great book to read for "normal" Christians (like me) who find it all too easy to either lose sight of God's global rescue plan, or else lose confidence in the part that I can usefully play."

DAN STEEL, Elder, Magdalen Road Church; Ministry Program
Director, Yarnton Manor, Oxford

"In a world that finds hope in anything and everything but Jesus, Jim offers a kingdom vision, a tangible invitation, and a helpful example for any disciple and every church to follow. This book will do more than just help you plant more churches or send more missionaries. In Jim's poignant reminders, I trust that you'll also find your role in planting the gospel and sending God's true hope—whether to neighbors or nations—in Christ alone."

BEN CONNELLY, Servant Leadership Team, Salt & Light
Community; Director, Plant Fort Worth and The Equipping Group

"This is a great book for all of us who are tempted to settle for a comfortable church life. We will catch a fresh excitement for our majestic mission and will be stirred up to see the part we can play."

JONTY ALLCOCK, Pastor, The Globe Church, London;
Author, *Impossible Commands*

"Mobility is an essential element in the mission of the church. Without it, we are swimming in sentimentality and dancing with disobedience. This book not only gives a biblical vision of gospel mission but wisdom and guidance from a pastor and church who are praying, giving, and going. Trust me, you want to learn from Jim. These pages are a testimony of what God has done—and can do for you. If you want to see members sent and churches planted for the name of Jesus, you are holding the right book."

J.A. MEDDERS, Co-author, *The Soul-Winning Church*; Director of Theology and Content, Send Network

"Page after page, I was encouraged, uplifted, and joyful about how God allows us to be a part of his cosmic purposes. With written excellence, Jim shows us how God sends his people to accomplish his task of kingdom-building. I found this book to be a thrilling explanation of why and how God sends his people. I commend it not only to church planters and vocational missionaries but to every Christian looking to understand how God works in accomplishing his purposes through his people."

BRIAN HOWARD, President, Acts 29

"*Send* is a grace-saturated treatment of the radical mission of the church to magnify Christ in the Great Commission. In a thorough but concise way, Jim Essian has given us an immensely encouraging work that both informs and inspires."

JARED C. WILSON, Assistant Professor of Pastoral Ministry, Midwestern Seminary; Author, *The Gospel-Driven Church*

"Practical, prophetic, and deeply pastoral—this book is a true gift to Christ's church. *Send* beautifully captures God's heart for the lost and underscores the urgency for the church to reflect his redemptive mission. Not merely a book to read once but a resource to be studied, absorbed, and woven into the fabric of our discipleship. As we engage with its wisdom, we are compelled to reset our posture toward the Great Commission, aligning ourselves afresh with the Spirit's leading in reaching the lost."

DR DOUG LOGAN JR., President, Grimké Seminary; Director of Urban Church Planter Development, Send Network

send

JIM ESSIAN

Send
Loving Your Church by Praying, Giving or Going
© 2024 Jim Essian

Published by:
The Good Book Company

thegoodbook.com | thegoodbook.co.uk
thegoodbook.com.au | thegoodbook.co.nz | thegoodbook.co.in

Original series cover design by Faceout Studio | Art direction and design by André Parker

ISBN: 9781802541014 | JOB-007877 | Printed in India

CONTENTS

To my wife, Heather,
my partner in life and ministry.

FOREWORD

BY JOBY MARTIN

As I write, the church that I have the joy of getting to pastor, The Church of Eleven22, is about to turn twelve years old. Looking back, I see so many faces and so many stories, some miraculous and some heartbreaking. I remember when we felt that God was calling us to launch our second campus back in 2015. I remember feeling challenged in January of 2020 that maybe we were missing a major opportunity to disciple people online, and launching that ministry only a week before the world shut down through Covid. It's wild to reflect on these twelve years of seeking God and finding him to be better than I could have ever imagined.

Before we planted Eleven22, I sat praying at the kitchen table with my wife, Gretchen, asking God if this was the next thing he had for us. Should we plant or should I take a job at an established church where I could plug into what God was already doing? How would we pay for things? What if it didn't work out? Gretchen, with her confidence in God and in me, is the real reason why we took that step out of the boat back in 2012. There's no way we could have known then what we know now, that more people worship in the churches that we've planted around the world than worship with us on a weekend. For sure, we've walked through some painful and difficult moments, but we've also experienced the power and presence of God in ways that are beyond comprehension.

I get asked often, what's the secret sauce of Eleven22? I've got one answer to share that I think Jim so powerfully walks out through this book: *we respond to the gospel.* I heard the gospel message as a 16-year-old at a pretty painful point in my life, and I've never recovered. I cannot get over the good news that Jesus lived the life I couldn't live, died that death that I deserve, and rose from the dead so that I could live eternally with him. News like that demands a response!

At Eleven22, I end every sermon the same way, calling people to respond to the gospel in one of three ways—we sing, we bring, and we pray. I think that's what Jim is also doing in this book. He's calling you, the reader, to respond to the gospel with your life.

We sing: The appropriate response to the message of Jesus' life, death, resurrection, and ascension is to worship God! When we understand that we were dead spiritually—that we were wretched, hard-hearted sinners—and that Jesus exchanged his perfect, holy, righteousness for us, how can we not sing? How can we not respond with overwhelming thankfulness? The gospel is good news because it's impossible for us to be restored to him in any other way. We find ourselves in the domain of darkness apart from Jesus. But God... But God did what we couldn't. God made a way where there wasn't. God paid the debt that we owed. It causes us to sing with our whole hearts:

And when I think that God, his Son not sparing,
Sent him to die, I scarce can take it in.
That on the cross, my burden gladly bearing,
He bled and died to take away my sin...
THEN SINGS MY SOUL...

What about you? When was the last time you responded to the glorious message of the cross and empty tomb with shouts of praise and declared him alone as worthy?

We bring: The appropriate response to the generous heart of God who sent his only Son for us is to give back to him what he has given to us. This is rooted in two truths. First, everything we have is from him. There is nothing that we own that didn't come from the hand of God. Second, we give our first and best because he gave his first and best. We aren't tipping God; we bring him the firstfruits of all that he's entrusted to us as an act of worship, because we've learned it from him.

Out of the overflow of perfect love that existed eternally within the Trinity, everything was created. Out of the overflow of perfect love that exists in the heart of God, the Son was sent. 1 John 4:19 simply says, "We love because he first loved us." The theologian John Stott puts it this way, "God does not love us because Christ died for us; Christ died for us because God loves us." God loved and God gave. What about you? You will give to what you love. Is it his mission and his kingdom that captures your heart, shapes your dreams, and how you steward what you own?

We pray: The appropriate response to the gospel is to run to God. We pray because we have a good heavenly Father who wants us to come to him. We have access to the throne! When Jesus was crucified, Matthew 27:51 tells us that the veil in the temple that protected the holy of holies was torn from top to bottom. This implies that it was God who tore the veil—it's God who has given us access to his throne through Christ. I love the quote from Tim Keller, "The only person who dares wake up a king at 3 a.m. for a glass of water is a child. We have that kind of access." You are his beloved child. You have access to the throne of God. What do you do with that access?

If we respond to the gospel, the gospel will advance. God's kingdom will flourish when we act on the challenges Jim presents in this book. The apostle Paul says, "You were bought at a price. Therefore honor God with your bodies" (1 Corinthians 6:20). Our response should be to go wherever he calls us and to give our lives for him so that others might know the good news.

Joby Martin
Pastor, The Church of Eleven22
Author, If the Tomb is Empty and Anything is Possible

1. GOD'S VISION FOR THE WORLD

For the earth will be filled with the knowledge of the glory of the LORD as the waters cover the sea.
Habakkuk 2:14

You are in the midst of a global movement.

A movement that is advancing in every culture and place, across the millennia—a Spirit-filled, gospel-armed people who will not stop or even slow down until we break through the gates of hell and welcome our King and his kingdom. We will not lose, because he has already won. It's a movement of grace and truth, of word and deed, and in the fear of the Lord, his church multiplies.

And you've been invited in.

We fear nothing and no man; we seek the glory of God and the good of all people. The gospel propels us forward with boldness and audacity. We can be the most entrepreneurial, courageous, and fearless people. Why?

Because Jesus was victorious. Because the kingdom is coming in its fullness.

All this is true. But it doesn't always *feel* or even *look* true. So let me show you how all this will end, because it ends in glory. And if we can see the finish line, maybe it can help us to see how the Spirit will get us there, and how we can join him on his mission.

IN THE DESERT

The world is broken. Ravaged by sin, torn apart in conflict, fractured. Technology broadcasts each fissure and sends it straight to our phones. More than any generation before us, we're inundated with knowledge, and so much of it demoralizes the heart and devastates the soul. We know more than we should know.

Anxiety (at least in the US) is at an all-time high,[1] and hope at an all-time low. Like an economic bear market, the situation seems dire and investors' confidence is low. We're pulling out all our cash and stuffing it under the mattress—this surely isn't the right time for planting churches, starting new initiatives, and thinking about multiplication. We can barely keep our friends in church (or in the faith), it seems.

The prophet Habakkuk felt the same way in his time, well over two millennia ago:

---

1 https://news.gallup.com/poll/505745/depression-rates-reach-new-highs.aspx (accessed February 12, 2024).

O LORD, how long shall I cry for help,
  and you will not hear?
Or cry to you "Violence!"
  and you will not save? (Habakkuk 1:2)

For Habakkuk, the world is a desert. The knowledge of God's glory has dried up. Habakkuk lives in a time when God's people are in a bad place. Assyria has taken over, deporting most of God's people and dominating those who remain in Jerusalem. God's people haven't been following him faithfully. There's violence and destruction, contention and injustice, conflict, scandal, and greed. Everyone is striving for the "Assyrian Dream" and following their heart wherever it leads. Things are getting really bad.

The Old Testament prophets usually speak in tumultuous times full of evil and injustice, when God's people are trying to figure out how to navigate the world. Maybe that's why they often read like a Radiohead song. Sometimes, I just want to give Jeremiah or Habakkuk a hug. And yet, they are filled with the promises of God.

Habakkuk is no false optimist. He looks around, dejected and depressed, and calls out to God, "How long shall I cry for help?" (v 2). *God, how long will this take?* Habakkuk wants answers and he pleads with God to do something. God does answer him, but not in a way that Habakkuk likes. God says he will do something about it, but first it's going to get worse before it gets better (v 5-11).

IS GOD BIG ENOUGH?

So Habakkuk prays again, "Are you not from everlasting?" (v 12). In English, these words don't necessarily come across as confrontational, but in the original Hebrew, it's a rhetorical question. He's crying out to God and saying, *What are you doing?!*

Habakkuk looks out at all the evil and brokenness around him and says, *I thought you were eternal; I thought you were big and powerful—why aren't you doing anything, God?*

Have you ever prayed like this? I don't know if I've ever been this audacious before God—but it moves me.

When I survey the landscape of my city, Fort Worth in Texas, I see the prosperity, growth and development, and yet how much is still broken. It's all thinly veiled with success and money and beauty and new buildings and another coffee shop—but so little glory. It doesn't matter how pretty or put-together the campus and students are at our local university. Every year, we minister to the brokenness of that campus: eating disorders, identity issues, doubt, date rape.

It doesn't matter how big our churches are or how nice our buildings look if they're often simply filled with bored churchgoers and gospel-less sermons, offering little more than a pat on the back and a Bible verse.

It doesn't matter how great our church programs or ministries are if there's a growing secularism in the city. Not only do people not give Jesus credit; they don't even find the ethos of Christianity credible. Our initiatives don't meet a felt need anymore.

I live in the most liberal neighborhood in North Texas. There are a lot of cool things about that, and a lot of things I agree with too, but in my neighborhood, you are more accepted if you're a witch than if you're a pastor. We're surrounded by all this brokenness and sin, and the land feels dry; like a drought of glory and grace. Is the church dependent enough on Jesus, empowered enough by the Spirit, secure enough in the Father's love? Are we desperate enough to pray enough for the glory and grace of Jesus to saturate our churches, our communities, and our hearts?

In a huge study in the US called "The Great Opportunity", the organizers found that "between 28 million and 42 million young people being raised in self-identified Christian homes will choose to leave a life with Christ over the next 30 years. That's the largest single generational loss in our country's history."[2] And why?

*It turns out that the vast majority of young people leaving the church have not done a deep intellectual study of truth claims and come up with a theological dissent with Christianity. **Most simply think a life with Jesus doesn't matter** [emphasis mine].*[3]

---

2 The Great Opportunity: The American Church in 2050, PDF, p 9.

3 https://www.thegospelcoalition.org/article/study-americas-greatest-gospel-opportunity-lives-in-your-house/ (accessed February 12, 2024).

Their idea of God is too small. We have made him "ignorable."[4]

Some of us grew up in youth groups and churches that only told us how God wanted us to live and how he could help us have a pretty good life. Just, you know, don't have sex before you're married and be nice. And perhaps few of us were told that God *is* life—that Jesus is enough. That the bigness and beauty of God is worth giving our lives to!

Here's what we can learn from Habakkuk: he sees evil and injustice, and he wonders where God is, but he doesn't tweet his frustrations, and he doesn't stop attending church services. He doesn't walk away from the faith; he prays! *His God is big enough to get mad at.* Habakkuk prays in his doubts because he believes God is big enough to do something about this mess!

In the midst of our hard times, political controversies, sexual-abuse scandals, and wrestling with our own doubts and struggles, we need a death-grip hold on the promises of God. And as we'll see, God promises Habakkuk something that we too can cling to.

THE VISION OF AN OASIS

The Atacama Desert is in Chile.[5] It's the driest place on earth, receiving just one millimeter of rain each

---

4 Ray Ortlund sermon, August 12th, 2012, Immanuel Church.

5 I first heard this illustration from Jon Tyson at the 2022 Exponential Conference. https://vimeo.com/693229757 (accessed February 12, 2024).

year. It's so dry that NASA runs test missions for Mars there. But just below the desert floor is an abundance of possibility. 200 varieties of flowers lie beneath the surface, and every five years or so, enough rain falls to create what's called a *superbloom*. In an eruption of color, the desert comes to life, full of glory.

The seeds are there—it just takes a little rain.

This is God's answer to Habakkuk's lament: "For the earth will be filled with the knowledge of the glory of the LORD as the waters cover the sea" (2:14). Just as scientists tell us the universe is constantly expanding, the earth will continuously erupt with the glory of God. God says, *I know you see all this evil and injustice, Habakkuk, but mark this down: here's how it all ends—my glory will fill the earth!*

The knowledge of God's goodness, beauty, power, love, justice, holiness, and grace will one day be ocean deep across the desert floor. *This is God's plan that we're caught up in!*

This is God's answer to Habakkuk and to us:

> *I know you have questions.*
> *I know you see the injustices in the world, and the brokenness around you.*
> *I know you're grieved by the abuse, the oppression, the sorrow, the struggles.*
> *I know you even have doubts, and sometimes it seems like I'm far away.*

I know you wonder sometimes if my promises are true.
But this is how it will end: my glory will fill the earth!

God's glory is the fullness and essence of who he is—it's God on display. And so, like the waters cover the seas, God's glory will be ocean deep on your campus, in your neighborhood, in your city. The knowledge of all that he is will saturate your nation, the 10-40 window[6], even the whole world. The calling on Adam and Eve to fill the earth, and the commission from Jesus to go and make disciples of all nations will be fulfilled.

What would happen if the glory of God was ocean deep in your family? What would happen if the glory of God was ocean deep in your church? What would happen if the glory of God was ocean deep in your neighborhood? If people knew the beauty of God and the grace of God and the goodness of God; if everyone knew and loved Jesus, what problems would that alleviate? What social ills would that solve? What divisions would that reconcile?

Everything that's broken will be restored. Every act of evil and sign of abuse, all oppression and injustice will be made right. Everything will be new again. The seeds are there, and the rain is coming.

Jesus gives the apostle John a fuller vision of this in Revelation:

---

6 A rectangular area covering Northern Africa, the Middle East and Asia, that includes some of the poorest countries and people groups who haven't been reached with the gospel message.

*And I heard a loud voice from the throne saying, Behold,
the dwelling place of God is with man. He will dwell
with them, and they will be his people, and God himself
will be with them as their God. He will wipe away every
tear from their eyes, and death shall be no more, neither
shall there be mourning, nor crying, nor pain anymore,
for the former things have passed away. And he who
was seated on the throne said, "Behold, I am making all
things new" ... And I saw no temple in the city, for its
temple is the Lord God the Almighty and the Lamb. And
the city has no need of sun or moon to shine on it, for
the glory of God gives it light, and its lamp is the Lamb.
(Revelation 21:3-5, 22-23)*

The seeds are there and the rain is coming... just wait till
you see the vivid colors of God's glory in full bloom.

A VISION THAT SENDS

How is God's glory coming? Through the church!
Through us. God's vision for the world is what sends us.
The church is drawn into this cosmic flood of his glory.
We see this in Ephesians:

*Now to him who is able to do far more abundantly than
all that we ask or think, according to the power at work
within us, to him be glory in the church and in Christ
Jesus throughout all generations, forever and ever.
Amen. (Ephesians 3:20-21)*

God is accomplishing this vision through his church—
through ordinary people like you and me. This has always

been his way: it's why the historian and sociologist Rodney Stark looked at the rapid multiplication of the church in the 1st and 2nd centuries and concluded, "The early church spread as ordinary people accepted it and then shared it with their families and friends, and the faith was carried from one community to another in this same way."[7]

In my city, food trucks are everywhere. Barbecue, popsicles, tacos, even French beignets! Who needs a restaurant when one parks right in your neighborhood? This is what the church is like: a mobile food truck sent into neighborhoods and cities to give hungry people food.

Do you want to see your city lavished by the grace of God? The whole place drenched with God's glory? What about college campuses? What about the nations? *Where is your heart drawn to?* What makes you cry out, *Are you not from everlasting?* It is to there you are sent. If you've caught a vision for what *should* be but isn't yet, that's the heart of God; go where he's sending you. If the glory of God will one day fill that place, don't you want to be a part of it?

And if the answer is *No, actually, if I'm being honest, I don't want to be a part of it, I'm not that moved by the idea of being sent—see, I'm busy. I can barely keep my room clean, I'm trying to get my life on track, first let me get married or have some children,* then I would love you to put this book

---

7 Rodney Stark, *The Triumph of Christianity* (HarperCollins, 2012), p 69.

down, pick up your Bible, flip to the end, find Revelation 21, and read the first four verses. The holy city, the bride adorned for her husband—that's the church. That's how it all ends.

If you're struggling to catch this vision, pray this prayer: *Jesus, will you give me a vision for what my city could look like if the knowledge of your glory covered it like the waters cover the seas? Amen.*

IN FAITH, LIVE SENT
It would be easy to feel discouraged looking out at the unending barrenness of the Atacama Desert, unaware of the seeds of florals waiting below the surface ready to burst and bloom their beauty. In the same way, you and I could take in the desert vista of the culture and church in our current moment and coil in, self-protecting (or maybe fight back in aggressive despair). But the Lord says to Habakkuk, "The righteous shall live by his faith" (Habakkuk 2:4).

How do we live by faith in these troubled times? We lift up our eyes to this vision for the future that God has given us. We trust that his word has gone out and will not return void (Isaiah 55:11). Our response to God's word is always to believe and obey. And he has told us how this ends. The only right response to God's vision for the world is to live *by faith*. This verse in Habakkuk is so vital that it's quoted three times in the New Testament (Romans 1:17; Galatians 3:11; Hebrews 10:38).

We live not by what we see, but by trusting in the wisdom of God. Not by our feelings or desires, but by God's promises.

We see a desert; God sees a superbloom ready to happen.

We see the church in decline, the Twitter wars, culture in constant conflict; God sees the readiness of revival.

This is an opportunity for a life of adventure, trusting in the promises of God. A Christian living by faith with a vision of God's glory should never be bored. J.D. Greear writes, "Whatever you're good at, do it well for the glory of God, and do it somewhere strategic for the mission of God."[8]

In faith, we are to live *sent*.

God has a vision for the world and he's inviting you in. The seeds lie waiting to bloom, the rain is coming; rise up and join the harvest.

ACTION STEPS

- Read through the book of Habakkuk, keeping an eye out for statements that show the prophet's honest despair, as well as those that show his confidence in the Lord.

- Look up your local online news outlet and contemplate whether any of the articles show

---

8 J.D. Greear, *Gaining By Losing: Why the Future Belongs to Churches that Send* (Zondervan, 2015), p 75.

evidence of brokenness in your community. Pray for these issues at your church small group or prayer meeting.

- Ask God to give you a vision of his glory. Pray that you would be able to look forward to the wonderful future we have as the family of God, and let it shape your daily walk with him.

2. GOD'S VISION FOR US

Peter, an apostle of Jesus Christ,
To those who are elect exiles of the Dispersion...
1 Peter 1:1

We find ourselves in the *Age of the Autonomous Self.*

The famous are our prophets.
The message preached is one of self-actualization, self-
achievement, and self-dependence.
The mystery to solve is to find yourself.
The greatest sin of our culture is not being true to
yourself.

This religion of self might be cloaked in karma or a vague
spirituality that eats, prays, and loves itself to "your best
life now." It may even be masked by church language,
but it's all the same. And it doesn't work. This solo quest
of "finding my true self" or "being true to myself" or
"recovering my inner child" is exhausting. I don't know
about you, but I get tired of myself.

For all the talk about the "self" in our culture, Jesus offers a far higher vision of you and the glory that you have (and will have). His gospel offers clean air. Pure oxygen—so breathe deep.

ELECT EXILES

The apostle Peter wrote a letter to a group of churches in what is now Turkey, addressing them as "elect exiles"— chosen strangers, saved and sent. This is your identity too. This is God's vision for us. The phrase "elect exiles" is key to understanding your whole life as a Christian. In just two words, Peter describes our relationship with God and our relationship with the world—how God sees us and our place in redemptive history. He distills what the apostle Paul explains in the first two chapters of his letter to the Ephesians—namely, that we were chosen before the foundations of the world, predestined for adoption, and graced to do the works he sent us to do in a world not yet our home. In Peter's next chapter he'll say we are "chosen and precious" (1 Peter 2:4). Who needs self-discovery when the Most High calls us his own?

To the world we are foreigners; but to God we are elect.

Culture may reject you; but God has chosen you.

The world will misunderstand you; but God knows you.

You don't feel like you have a place; but God has adopted you into his house.

Do you realize how much confidence that gives us? How

much courage and comfort it promises us in the face of anything? It's stunning, if you think about it.

We have a relationship with God and a relationship with the world. The big question is this: which one defines the other? It's a diagnostic question that pierces the heart, because we know the Sunday-school answer but our lives might testify differently.

We tend to like this world. A lot. It's really not so bad: this world has breakfast tacos and Bordeauxs and barbecue and baseball—it's a good time to be alive. But we have to reevaluate how much we love what the world loves, values, and celebrates (even the great things), and bring that in line with a passionate and public faith that loves and trusts Jesus above everything else. Often, we've fallen in love with the world without realizing it. And more importantly, we haven't realized that it hinders our affection for Jesus and our knowledge of his affection for us. As Christianity becomes less and less popular and influential in the West, we're going to have to be more and more bold and courageous—our relationship with the world is going to have to change. If "elect" defines your relationship to God, "exiles" defines your relationship to the world. You are not home. Maybe it shouldn't feel too comfortable here.

STRANGERS IN A STRANGE LAND
Peter pens this epistle to the "Dispersion" (1:1)—literally to those *scattered* about in what is modern-day Turkey.

Pontus, Galatia, Cappadocia, Asia, and Bithynia was a geographical area about the size of California, and it had the diversity of California too. He's addressing many different cultures and ethnicities in urban places full of urban people who breathe in the culture of the Roman Empire as well as the sub-cultures of these various cities.

It's possible that some of these Christians were literally exiles—refugees from Rome; the Emperor Claudius sent Christians out of Rome a few times. Persecution was heating up—they weren't being fed to the lions quite yet, but opposition was rising.

Peter is also describing their relationship to the culture they've been sent to. These Christians live encircled by progressive ideas, are offered a pantheon of gods to worship, and confront cultural habits and practices deeply embedded in the rhythms of the native people. Technology is advancing with the Roman road—the world is beginning to become more global, bringing new ideas, new styles, and new ways of thinking. "Exiles" is a socio-spatial metaphor; the recipients of his letter are strangers in their communities because they are citizens of heaven living on earth. When you become a Christian your whole life changes. You're not just adding a new element to your life; your entire existence shifts. It's a complete transformation. When you've experienced the grace and glory of God, the gospel has collided with your heart and changed you from the inside out.

And so, like a refugee—like a foreigner—people in the surrounding culture look at you differently and treat you differently. Maybe they reject you or mock you. Certainly, you don't fit in.

One time, all the elders at my church went on a hunt in West Texas. When you think of the state of Texas, what you're probably picturing is West Texas: cowboy boots, guns, cattle, big belt buckles, the Texas sky. On our way back to Fort Worth, we stopped at a famous diner—the best-chicken-fried-steak-in-the-world kind of place. There was Pastor Brent who loves hunting and fishing, and my buddy Dustin who was our guide. He has guns and a boat and a big truck—he's that guy. But the rest of us... well, let's just say we did not fit in.

There was Pastor AJ and Pastor Matt, all tattooed up, wearing black. There was Pastor Kaynenn, who *is* black. And then me: an Armenian from Detroit—the Motor City. Motown. The land of Eminem and the White Stripes. In other words, not country at all. I hate bugs. My wife had to remove the dead possum from the garage that one time... This was the group who walked into that famous West Texas diner, and the whole place in their hats and boots stopped and looked at us, like that movie moment where all the chatter and clinking of forks and knives dies down as everyone stares.

Being an elect exile feels a bit like this. Except that the stakes are often higher than receiving a few stares and feeling a bit awkward.

There's an Iranian judge, Mohammad Moghiseh, who is known as the Judge of Death. He hates Christians. In October 2020 he sentenced four men to ten years in prison because they started a church in their homes: "Your actions are worthy of death," he proclaimed.[9] On the day you're reading this, Christians around the world are being sent to prison. In fact, today, there will be brothers and sisters who are sentenced to death, just for what they believe. In the West, there will be believers today who lose out on finances, relationships, and political capital, solely because they claim Christ as Lord.

Exiles are, by definition, unsettled, uncomfortable, and usually, unsafe.

So if our citizenship is in heaven, and if being an exile here is hard, *why are we here?*

SCATTERED WITH A PURPOSE

Remember Habakkuk from the last chapter—he was lamenting the exile of God's people in the Assyrian Empire. God comforts him with a vision of his glory covering the whole earth, not just Jerusalem.

Well, we can see something Habakkuk couldn't see— that exile was part of the way God began to cover the earth with his glory, with people calling on his name for salvation. We can look in the rearview mirror of history

---

9 https://www.ugchristiannews.com/iran-judge-to-christian-converts-your-actions-are-worthy-of-death/ (accessed February 12, 2024).

and see what Habakkuk couldn't understand. The exile of God's people from their land meant that, by the time of Jesus' birth, they were scattered throughout the Roman Empire.

Because of the exile, every city in the ancient world had synagogues—a local community worshiping the one true God, a witness to the God of Abraham, Isaac, and Jacob. Because of their presence, some Gentiles also came to worship God. So when the early church began to spread, the gospel multiplied rapidly, sometimes among Jews, often among these Gentile "God-fearers," and it was through them that Christianity spread through the world.

Not only that but everyone in the eastern half of the Roman Empire spoke Greek—a legacy of the empire Alexander the Great had built, and the Greek-ruled states that followed before the Romans swept in. Therefore, gospel preaching and gospel letter-writing could be in a language everyone grasped. And because of the Pax Romana—the "Peace of Rome"—travel was fairly easy and reasonably safe—Christianity could begin to go global.

In other words, this succession of dominant world powers—the Assyrians and the Babylonians and the Greeks and the Romans—was part of the way God brought about the conditions for his gospel to spread rapidly, through the lives and words of his elect exiles.

Our exile has a purpose: it is the mission of God to cover this world with knowledge of him and faith in him. Christopher Wright says, "God's mission is what fills the gap between the scattering of the nations in Genesis 12 and the healing of the nations in Revelation 22."[10] The New City Catechism captures our sent-ness in its answer to the question, "What is the Church?":

> *God chooses and preserves for himself a community elected for eternal life and united by faith, who love, follow, learn from, and worship God together. **God sends out this community** [emphasis mine] to proclaim the gospel and prefigure Christ's kingdom by the quality of their life together and their love for one another.*[11]

THE FEAR OF GOD

But what will sustain elect exiles and keep us moving out with the gospel rather than fearfully staying out of trouble as much as we can?

Put simply, it's this: fear. But it's fear of a different kind.

In Acts 9, after the first outbreak of persecution (Acts 8:1-8) had seen the first Christians sent out from Jerusalem and boldly witnessing to all they met, "the church throughout all Judea and Galilee and Samaria had [a brief time of] peace and was being built up. And

---

10 Christopher J. H. Wright, *The Mission of God: Unlocking the Bible's Grand Narrative* (InterVarsity Press, 2006), p 455.

11 Question 48 in *The New City Catechism*, (Crossway, 2017), p 114-115.

walking in the fear of the Lord and in the comfort of the Holy Spirit, it multiplied" (Acts 9:31).

Here's the calculation we glean from that verse:

Fear of God + Comfort of God = Multiplication

Certainly, the early exiled Christians were afraid, but they feared God more. This idea—to fear God—is throughout the Bible; the fear of the Lord is the beginning of wisdom. The preacher in Ecclesiastes ends the book by saying, "The end of the matter is: fear God" (12:13, AMP). At the beginning of his book *Rejoice and Tremble,* Michael Reeves writes:

> *I want you to rejoice in this strange paradox that the gospel both frees us from fear and gives us fear. It frees us from our crippling fears, giving us instead a most delightful, happy, and wonderful fear.*[12]

The fear of God is a bit like standing on a cliff overlooking the ocean at sunset. It's beautiful, it's magisterial, it's huge—it's so wholly beyond you, outside of you, bigger than you. In that moment, you're not stressed out about work—it's impossible. In that moment, you're not worried what other people think about you—you're not thinking about yourself at all. You are in a completely self-forgetful place because the only thing that matters is how big and beautiful your view is and how you don't want to fall in.

---

12 Michael Reeves, *Rejoice and Tremble* (Crossway, 2021), p 16.

Elect exiles fear the Lord. We join with Moses in exile from Egypt, who took his shoes off when standing on holy ground. We are alongside the disciples who trembled at Jesus even more than at the storm, because he has power over the wind and waves. We resonate with the writer of Hebrews, who says it is a fearful thing to fall into the hands of the living God (Hebrews 10:31).

Simply, the fear of God is the very thing you were made for: to be fully alive in the presence of God, while at the same time completely unashamed and self-forgetful. You realize your vulnerability and your limitations, but there's no insecurity or anxiety at all. The cross of Christ has covered you; you're free to just be in awe of him now.

So we fear God. But at the same time, there's a nearness to God.

THE COMFORT OF THE HOLY SPIRIT

The Holy Spirit is God: the third Person of the Trinity. When Jesus was with his disciples during his three-year earthly ministry, he told them that they would do even greater things than he was doing (John 14:12). He was going to send them the Holy Spirit. After his death and resurrection and then his ascension, he did (Acts 2); the fire of the church was lit and the rest is history. Without the Spirit the church is nothing.

It's the Holy Spirit who opened your eyes to the truth of Jesus.

It's the Holy Spirit who dwells within you.

It's the Holy Spirit who convicts you of sin.

It's the Holy Spirit who unites you to Jesus, and us to one another.

And it's the work of the Holy Spirit that empowers us, guides us, and comforts us on the mission of God we have been called to.

This word "comfort" in the original language is the same word Jesus employs to describe the Holy Spirit in John 14 and 15—*paraclete*. It's a combination of two words: *para*, to come alongside, and *kaleo*, to call. The Spirit walks with you and speaks to you.

This is what comforts us. I've spoken with dozens of church members who are moving away—folks that are graduating from school or their work is taking them away from our city and church—and the conversation is usually the same each time. The Lord has done something special in them while they were here, but they're nervous about how life will affect them in a different place, a different community, a different church. And so I remind them: it's the Spirit that did all that work! And the Spirit goes with them! The Spirit is the Comforter, the primary discipler in the life of every Christian.

When the church is "in the comfort of the Holy Spirit" (Acts 9:31), it's a dynamite place to be:

- The Comforter empowers us: "But you will

receive power when the Holy Spirit has come upon you, and you will be my witnesses in Jerusalem and in all Judea and Samaria, and to the end of the earth" (Acts 1:8).

- The Spirit makes us bold: "And when they had prayed, the place in which they were gathered together was shaken, and they were all filled with the Holy Spirit and continued to speak the word of God with boldness" (4:31).

- The Helper gives us wisdom: "But they could not withstand the wisdom and the Spirit with which he was speaking" (6:10).

- The Counselor will send us to share the gospel with people: "And the Spirit said to Philip, 'Go over and join this chariot'" (8:29).

Even more, the Spirit:

- gives us passion in our mission (19:21).

- stops us from going somewhere (16:7).

- fills us with faith (11:24).

- fills us with joy (13:52).

- sends out church planters (13:2).

- prepares us for future suffering (20:23).

- but then gives us the strength to face it anyway (20:22).

Notice, however, that the Spirit doesn't comfort us by taking us out of the uncomfortable situation. We're still exiles—it's uncomfortable. In fact, the Spirit will often lead us *into* situations that are uncomfortable, and where we'll need to find comfort from him.

God doesn't make us more comfortable; *he is* our comfort. The Spirit isn't someone who brings you a blanket; *he is* the blanket. He doesn't bring you water; *he is* the water.

Fear + Comfort = Multiplication

The result of truly knowing the fear and the comfort of God is that the church multiplies. The church isn't a safe place. But it is an exciting one.

THE CHURCH MULTIPLIES

I named my youngest daughter, Hadden, after the great (though not very cute) Baptist preacher, Charles Haddon Spurgeon. The "Prince of preachers" once said, "The Christian Church was designed from the first to be aggressive."[13] Jesus said that hell's gates won't hold us back (Matthew 16:18). Being in the comfort of the Spirit with the fear of God is like being in the eye of a hurricane or like a kite caught up in the wind—we're a part of something so much bigger than ourselves.

We are all part of God's mission. This is the power of God to save sinners for his glory through the ministry

---

13 Charles Spurgeon, "Metropolitan tabernacle statistics" in *The Sword and the Trowel, Volume I*, (April 1865), p 66.

of a broken yet redeemed people. This is the inbreaking of divine love piercing hard hearts; this great mercy that puts everything broken back together—and we're along for the ride!

Consider how Jesus prayed for you right before his arrest in the garden: "I do not ask that you take them out of the world, but that you keep them from the evil one ... As you sent me into the world, so I have sent them into the world" (John 17:15-18). Cultural Christianity lives settled; exiled Christians live sent. In his great book *Delighting in the Trinity*, Michael Reeves talks of joining Jesus in his sent-ness:

> *For when Jesus sends us, he is allowing us to share the missional, generous, outgoing shape of God's own life. The writer of Hebrews puts it like this: "Jesus also suffered outside the city gate [that is, he went out beyond where the people of God are] to make the people holy through his own blood. Let us, then, go to him outside the camp" (Heb 13:12-13). In other words, Jesus is found out there, in the place of rejection. That is where the Father has sent him, that he might bring sinners back as children. The Christian life is one of being where he is, of joining in how he has been sent.*[14]

The Christian life is one of being where he is. Not with the in-crowd; not with the picture-perfect life; not financially secure, settled, and comfortable. We are elect

14 Michael Reeves, *Delighting in the Trinity* (InterVarsity Press, 2012), p 105-106.

exiles. Chosen and precious. Sent and suffering. Walking in the fear of God and in the comfort of the Spirit, multiplying for his glory. There's nothing boring about it. We may suffer for it, as Jesus did, but above all, we are with him.

ACTION STEPS

- Think through some of the things that you love most in our world. Is it possible that you are too attached to any of them?

- Do you ever feel awkward, uncomfortable, or exposed because of standing out for your faith in Jesus? How can you reframe your thinking by seeing yourself as an "elect exile"?

- Look up the World Watch List from the international charity Open Doors to see a ranking of countries where Christians are most persecuted. Select one or two and particularly pray for your brothers and sisters there.

3. CHURCH PLANTING

Go therefore and make disciples of all nations, baptizing them in the name of the Father and of the Son and of the Holy Spirit, teaching them to observe all that I have commanded you. And behold, I am with you always, to the end of the age.
Matthew 28:19-20

My church started in our living room in 2010 in the heat of a Texan summer. Eight of us sat on couches dreaming of a new gospel work, and we launched weekly gatherings on January 9th 2011.

But it all started long before that.

History tells us that around 42 AD, Mark planted the first church outside of Jerusalem in Alexandria, Egypt—probably in a living room too. Seven years later, the apostle Paul went to Turkey, and a couple of years after that to Greece. In 52 AD, the apostle Thomas headed to India, armed with the Spirit and the gospel. In 66 AD, Bartholomew preached the gospel in Armenia—where my ancestors lived on my father's side.

And the church has never stopped advancing.

In 174 AD, the first Christians were reported in what today is Austria. By 280 AD, the gospel was being proclaimed in Northern Italy. By 350 AD, 31.7 million people claimed Christ as Lord in the Roman Empire—roughly 53% of the population. In 432 AD, Patrick headed to Ireland to plant churches (and my mom's side of the family celebrates this by drinking lots of green beer every March 17th!).

Two hundred years later, the first Christian missionaries arrived in China. A hundred years after that, Irish monks reached Iceland. In 900 AD, missionaries reached Norway. In 1498, the first Christians were reported in Kenya. In 1554, there were 1,500 converts to Christ in what's now called Thailand. In 1743, David Brainerd started a ministry and mission to the native Americans.

And the kingdom continued to burst forth.

In 1869, 13 people formed First Baptist Church of Lewisville, Texas. A hundred years later, they planted The Village Church, in Highland Village, Texas.[15] In 2006, The Village Church planted CityView Church in Keller, Texas. In 2011, CityView Church planted The Paradox Church (me!) in Downtown Fort Worth, Texas. And since 2016, we've planted five more churches in our family of churches, all just a few miles from each other.

---

15 I first heard a version of this in a sermon from Matt Chandler.

Why? Because the gospel is always on the move and God is always sending. Here's Spurgeon's take:

> *The Christian Church was designed from the first to be aggressive. It was not intended to remain stationary at any period, but to advance onward until its boundaries became commensurate with those of the world. It was to spread from Jerusalem to all Judea, from Judea to Samaria, and from Samaria unto the uttermost part of the earth. It was not intended to radiate from one central point only; but to form numerous centres from which its influence might spread to the surrounding parts. The plan was to plant Churches in all the great cities and centres of influence in the known world.*[16]

The gospel has been handed down to us as a legacy—a lineage of grace. And now, it's our turn.

THE BIBLICAL STRATEGY

The primary biblical strategy for expanding the gospel is church planting.

Now, likely you won't be a church-plant leader who's been called and sent out to start a new church (though you might!). But maybe you could be a part of a church-planting core team; maybe you could champion church-planting at your current church; or maybe if you

---

16 Charles Spurgeon, "Metropolitan tabernacle statistics" in *The Sword and the Trowel, Volume I*, (April 1865), p 66.

graduate or move location for some reason, you could consider being a part of a new church that doesn't have it all together yet instead of the established church down the road.

Fifteen years ago, I didn't even know you could start a new church. I don't know where I thought churches came from—maybe the church stork just dropped the little baby church off one day. But church planting is the New Testament strategy for making disciples:

> And Jesus came and said to them, "All authority in
> heaven and on earth has been given to me. Go therefore
> and make disciples of all nations, baptizing them
> in the name of the Father and of the Son and of the
> Holy Spirit, teaching them to observe all that I have
> commanded you. And behold, I am with you always, to
> the end of the age." (Matthew 28:18-20)

The famous words of the Great Commission are probably somewhat familiar to you. The risen Jesus stands in the midst of his apostles (a Greek term that literally means "sent one") and declares himself triumphant. The Father has given him every authority—the author of everything owns all things. He also promises that he will always be with us—never forsaking or leaving us. What great fear and great comfort! All authority and all presence! These bookended truths give us the confidence to do what he commands us to do: make disciples. And Jesus tells us how:

1. Go! (We are sent!)

2. To all nations (since his authority knows no bounds, our mission is ignorant to boundaries and risks and fears too).

3. Baptizing (this is the entrance into the church).

4. Teaching them to observe God's commands (this is how God's people live).

Tim Keller notes that we can only fulfill Jesus' Great Commission by planting churches, because teaching and baptism imply that new believers are incorporated into a covenant community.[17] "In other words, Jesus did not intend his disciples to go about haphazardly evangelizing; he instructed them to gather these new converts into new churches. So Paul tells Titus, 'The reason I left you in Crete was that you might put in order what was left unfinished and appoint elders in every town, as I directed you' (Titus 1:5 [NIV]). The appointment of elders also implies organized churches."[18]

This is precisely how the apostles interpreted the Great Commission; you only have to read the book of Acts to see it in action. The apostle Paul's church planting strategy was to introduce the gospel in a city through evangelism, plant the new disciples into a community of

17 https://redeemercitytocity.com/articles-stories/why-plant-churches (accessed February 12, 2024).

18 J.D. Greear, Gaining By Losing: Why the Future Belongs to Churches that Send (Zondervan, 2015), p 222.

believers, and develop leaders to serve the new church plant:

> *When they had preached the gospel to that city and had made many disciples, they returned to Lystra and to Iconium and to Antioch, strengthening the souls of the disciples, encouraging them to continue in the faith, and saying that through many tribulations we must enter the kingdom of God. And when they had appointed elders for them in every church, with prayer and fasting they committed them to the Lord in whom they had believed. (Acts 14:21-23)*

WHY PLANT NEW CHURCHES?

Starting new churches where none exist made sense when the gospel message was hitting cities for the first time—but why plant new churches now? If you aren't living in the United States, you might not be asking this question. There isn't a church on every corner in Iran or Uganda or China. And there may not be an abundance of healthy, gospel-preaching churches around you if you're in Brazil or the UK or Mexico. Planting new churches in those countries might seem more obvious and necessary—and our missions efforts should be church-planting efforts![19] But for now, I want to answer the question of why we should plant new churches even in seemingly church-saturated cities or nations—even in Texas, even in the US.

---

19 We'll cover more about global church planting in the next chapter.

CHURCHES CLOSING AND POPULATION GROWING

In 2018, a US study called "The Great Opportunity" was published. Based on the data, they came to this conclusion:

Since many churches have a lifespan of about 70 to 100 years, and since many of the Baby Boomer churches were planted in the early 1950s, we expect a significant wave of church closures in the near future. Church planting is near an all-time low on a per-capita basis; we need to triple church planting within the next five to ten years to meet the need.[20]

A year later, Lifeway Research found out they were right. "In 2019, approximately 3,000 Protestant churches were started in the U.S., but 4,500 Protestant churches closed."[21] Just five years before, those numbers were reversed. And the statistics post-pandemic will be worse.

Granted, some churches need to close—they aren't biblically faithful and Jesus rightfully snuffs their lampstand out (see Revelation 2 and 3). Or instead, church revitalization becomes a great gospel alternative to church planting. God may call some believers to step into a dying church to bring new life and ministry. Still, however you cut it, there are not enough biblically faithful churches to reach the lost. More churches are being uprooted than planted.

---

20 https://www.greatopportunity.org/starting-more-churches (accessed February 12, 2024).

21 https://research.lifeway.com/2021/05/25/protestant-church-closures-outpace-openings-in-u-s/ (accessed February 12, 2024).

Churches are closing, not enough churches are being planted, and the population is rising. The U.S. Census Bureau measured population growth from 23.2 million in 1850 to 330.2 million in 2020. This is expected to continue, with the population projected to reach 400 million by 2050. In the past, the church has kept pace with these growing numbers by planting new churches. From 1860 to 1906, U.S. Protestant churches planted one new church for every increase of 350 in the population, bringing the ratio by the start of World War I to one church for every 430 persons. In the decade after WWII, there was a large spike in church planting in the United States. The current lifespan of a church, however, is roughly 80-120 years. According to "The Great Opportunity" survey, we need to plant 8,000 new churches per year in the US alone to bridge the gap between church closures and population increase.

CHANGING CULTURAL TIDES AND BOLD EVANGELISM

Established churches (and established Christians) are typically more, well, established. They've done church a certain way for so long that any sort of social shifts can present a missional roadblock. Perhaps they don't ruffle any cultural feathers or stir any political pots because they aren't really a part of that conversation—they were planted during a different time, in a different type of garden, with different types of weeds, and they keep on doing church in the way they know how. This is a challenge to any established church, and we should fight to stay on mission in the changing cultural tides while simultaneously holding onto the unchanging truth of the gospel.

New churches, however, have no choice but to learn how to evangelize in the current cultural moment. As society changes, so do the needs and questions of the people. Sometimes cultural shifts require new churches, planted around different kinds of weeds, that can speak the gospel into new contexts.

For example, when we started just twelve years ago, questions around gender, women in leadership, abortion, and so on, were understood to be up for debate. But now, people are surprised to hear that there is a debate! They assume that what they learn from the pervading secular culture is the norm. Twelve years ago, our churches might have spoken of the immorality of the culture around us—but now, it's the culture around us that thinks we are immoral!

We see this in the early church too. As the Gentiles received the gospel, new questions and debates sprouted up with these new churches in Galatia and Macedonia and in other places. Acts 15 and most of the Pauline epistles address these challenges. My point is this: planting new churches is the best way to reach new cultures.

There is a danger in this, however. In an effort to convert the surrounding culture, new churches can find that the culture converts them instead. The stiff, traditional, Bible-teaching church up the road might be too risk-averse and comfortable with how things are, but better that than a new, edgy church plant that has been colonized by the culture, never actually reaching it. Don't let the world gentrify your spiritual heart after you move into the neighborhood with your hopes of missional cultural engagement. It's the light that overcomes the darkness, not the other way around.

GEOGRAPHIC INTENTIONALITY AND URBANIZATION

According to the United Nations, 68% of the world's population will live in urban areas by 2050. This trend is not limited to the United States—there's a global movement to the city. God is moving people and the church must move too.

Of course, God also loves the suburbs and rural areas. And in Fort Worth, we've seen a huge benefit to planting from the city out to the surrounding neighborhoods and towns. Being intentional about contextualizing ministry for your geographic location makes gospel work more effective. As our younger members got married and started having kids, they would move out from the city center, sent into new neighborhoods on mission with strollers and car seats in tow. They traded their bars and coffee shops for soccer games and PTA meetings—but their gospel witness never changed. Planting churches in suburban and rural areas is both necessary and effective in reaching the whole family. Each church can now minister to their communities in a way that is specific to the needs of the people they reach—still infused with the missional DNA of the sending church.

However, planting new churches in cities is still the greatest need. God loves people, and cities, by definition, have a lot of people. "I have many in this city who are my people," God says to Paul in Acts 18:10, and he says it to me and to you too. Often, the people in the city are the ones stirring the waters that change the cultural tides. Every sphere—business, art, education, government, media, finance, tech—finds its upstream home in the city, flowing out to the rest of the world. Church planter Paul would go to the public squares and gathering places in the heart of a city first, and reason about the resurrection with anyone who would listen. And some folk who listened had great influence and social connections (see Acts 17).

So we plant churches because more are needed to keep up with church closures and population growth; we plant churches because they are typically more effective in reaching a radically changing culture; and we plant churches to intentionally contextualize our gospel witness to the whole world, especially in cities where there is the most need and the most opportunity.

THE SENDING AND THE SENT
The last question we need to ask is how? As a church member and as church leaders, how do we start to consider this great work?

I started reading books on raising tweens and the challenges that arise as they grow up into adolescence when my daughter turned eleven. One comment in particular stuck out to me, in a book aptly titled, *How to Hug a Porcupine* (let the parent who has ears to hear understand!). The author was talking about the change my daughter was going through—the metamorphosis that's happening as she learned how to be a big girl with big-girl emotions and big-girl independence. It explained that my parenting when she was younger was sufficient for who she was then, but not for who she was becoming right now. The sentence I highlighted was this: "You too must go through a metamorphosis."[22]

This is true in church planting also—as the parent church prepares and releases the new plant, it will have to change too. How the sending church thinks about people and leaders and money and ministry will need to change. There's no formula or template in parenting— every kid is different. In the same way, we don't plant churches with a cookie-cutter. Every sending church and every church-planting team is different. They have different needs, different personalities, different gift combinations, different challenges. But there are a few anchors we can hold onto when thinking about being a church that plants other churches.

---

22 Julie A. Ross, *How to Hug a Porcupine* (McGraw Hill, 2008), p 6.

ANCHOR #1: FOSTER A SENDING CULTURE

A church-planting church needs a sending culture. Multiply and send everything! We don't just commission new churches but also new leaders for church groups and even graduating students—whoever is heading somewhere new, they're intentionally sent out. We have a "sent" class for our college seniors to prepare them for life after graduation. At our church, we bring all these different people to the front, lay hands on them, pray over them, and send them out. Eventually people get the picture: we're a sending church!

How can you champion and support a sending culture at your church?

ANCHOR #2: CHURCHES PLANT CHURCHES

The whole church should be involved in planting a new church. This can't just be the work of the lead pastor or missions director. 1 Corinthians 12 says that the church, like a body, is made up of all sorts of different parts and gifts—so when the church multiplies, it requires the whole body.

When church plants have gone out from our church, we make sure that the new team meets with every ministry in the church for training and mentoring. They talk with and train in kids' ministry, music ministry, connections, communications, and so on. The people who are going with the new church plant take three months off from volunteering on our teams to give them a reprieve and help with the transition to the hard work of serving in the new church. The whole church has to step up and help plant this new gospel work.

How can you intentionally be involved in supporting a church-planting team in your local congregation?

ANCHOR #3: BE FIERCELY GENEROUS WITH EVERYTHING

If we have a scarcity mindset in the kingdom of God, with a focus on all that we lack, we won't be ready to plant churches (or do much of anything). Jesus has a bunch of money and people and leaders in his back pocket—an abundance of whatever we will need to both plant a church and to be a sending church.

When a church plant goes out, its core team will often include many of the most committed members of the sending church—the top givers, the best leaders, the most dedicated volunteers. Most of the people that will go be a part of a church plant will be faithful people who've caught the vision—they're all in for the kingdom, and they want to see the mission of God advance. When we plant, we tell the planting pastor that everyone in the church is fair game to recruit—we aren't going to try to grasp and hold on to anyone.

We've sent out over 250 people and six elders from our church. But here's the thing: every time, it only took a few months until our attendance was right back up to where it had been; the giving was replenished just a few months after that, and the Spirit always raised up more elders. Default to being extraordinarily generous, and trust Jesus to provide.

Be open handed with your money, your people and your equipment. I remember when we were starting, I met with a large church in the city to ask for support. They took me on a tour of their premises, and there were literally 100 flat screens on the walls throughout their facility. They had a huge storage room with equipment—and they offered me nothing. Then, one small church gave us a torn screen, another church gave us a wobbly stage, another gave us an old projector, and it was such a blessing!

Do you have a scarcity or an abundance mindset, and how does that affect your generosity in the kingdom of God?

ANCHOR #4: FIGHT FOR CLARITY

They say it takes someone seven times before they actually hear you—before what you say sticks. There's no formula for church planting, but clarity does have a formula:

Clarity = Trust + Overcommunication

With our first church plant, we sent out one of my closest friends, Ryan. He had come to the church and was a faithful member, then he became a leader, a member of staff, and then our first elder. We had four years of friendship and history together, but still we needed to have dozens of conversations around his calling, his giftings, and his desires to plant a church. This was the first time we'd planted, so we were learning along the way, but it took several Google docs and whiteboards and conversations over lunch to get to a point of clarity around what this daughter church would look like.

Relationships are everything: relationships will cover a multitude of church-planting sins. Healthy, communicative relationships are the only way to battle against unspoken expectations, fear of man, fear of failure, fear of looking incompetent, trust issues—all those things that seep into our communication with one another, like a dirty filter. Trust is built in very small moments. It takes a long time to establish and it's easily lost, so you have to fight for it.

Positive overcommunication also takes time to develop. It requires both formal, written communication, and organic, coffee-table communication. Think about how much time Paul spent with Timothy and how much thought and prayer went into his communication to him. He was intentional, not distant or general, but affectionate and specific with him—even telling him to drink some more wine for his health (1 Timothy 5:23)!

How can you help to build trust and fight for clarity in your church?

A GOSPEL LEGACY

Your individual church may or may not be around 100 or so years from now, but the kingdom will still be advancing. The Spirit will still be moving, Jesus will be displaying his power, and the glory of God will one day cover the earth like the waters cover the seas. That's what you're invited into. That's the legacy that you get to be a part of. Church planting puts you on the front lines to see Jesus flex—to see his power on display in the lives of his people. It's hard and messy and amazing and worth it. The gospel of grace has been handed down to us as a legacy—and now it's our turn.

ACTION STEPS

- Use the Acts 29 website to read impact stories from church plants all over the world (acts29.com/stories). Pray for one or two of the teams you read about.

- Ask someone who has been at your church for a long time about the church's history, the changes they've seen, and what God has taught them.

- Look again at the four anchors of a sending church. Consider which of these values your church embodies or lacks and which you could pray into.

4. THE GLOBAL GOD

By your blood you ransomed people for God from every
tribe and language and people and nation.
Revelation 5:9

In Communist Romania, persecuted Christians would be tied up to crosses and smeared with human waste. It was illegal to preach the gospel, and pastors were being arrested left and right. But that didn't stop the church.

One particular pastor, Josef Tson, was threatened with death unless he stopped preaching. This is what happened on his arrest:

"Sir, let me explain how I see this issue," he said.
"Your supreme weapon is killing. My supreme weapon
is dying... Here is how it works. You know that my
sermons on tape have spread all over the country. If
you kill me, those sermons will be sprinkled with my
blood. Everyone will know I died for my preaching. And
everyone who has a tape will pick it up and say, 'I'd
better listen again to what this man preached, because

he really meant it; he sealed it with his life.' So, sir, my sermons will speak ten times louder than before. I will actually rejoice in this supreme victory if you kill me."

The interrogator sent him home. Later he heard from another pastor friend who had been arrested that another officer told him, "We know that Mr. Tson would love to be a martyr, but we are not that foolish to fulfill his wish."

Tson thought about that statement. Reflecting on the years of ministry where he kept a low profile, afraid of dying, but now placing his life on the altar, he was ready to die for the sake of the Gospel. "They were telling me they would not kill me! I could go wherever I wanted in the country and preach whatever I wanted, knowing I was safe. As long as I tried to save my life, I was losing it. Now that I was willing to lose it, I found it."[23]

What is it that gives men and women that kind of boldness to preach the gospel in the face of death?

In 1555, the Reformers John Bradford and John Leaf were being tied to the stake because of their love for Jesus. Turning to his fellow martyr, Bradford said, "Be of good comfort, brother; for we shall have a merry supper with the Lord this night."[24]

---

23 https://www.baptistpress.com/resource-library/news/romanian-josef-tson-recounts-gods-grace-amid-suffering/ (accessed February 12, 2024).

24 https://www.evangelical-times.org/john-bradford-the-martyr-who-dared-to-die-for-doctrine/ (accessed February 12, 2024).

What gives men and women that kind of peace and joy when confronting certain death?

Or how about the apostle Paul? "To live is Christ, and to die is gain," he wrote while imprisoned, chained, and guarded round the clock (Philippians 1:21). Where does that kind of courage come from? In a day when we're so easily offended, when we're so easily afraid—and when we're so afraid of offending; in a time when we're so incredibly self-protective and self-focused, what drives men and women to lose their lives in order to gain them?

I think it comes from a deep-seated belief that Jesus is everything—that Jesus is worthy even of our lives. A conviction that *life* is nothing without Jesus and *death* is nothing because of Jesus. It's because of visions like this one in Revelation 5:

> *And they sang a new song, saying, "Worthy are you to take the scroll and to open its seals, for you were slain, and by your blood you ransomed people for God from every tribe and language and people and nation, and you have made them a kingdom and priests to our God, and they shall reign on the earth." (Revelation 5:9-10)*

HE IS WORTHY

The book of Revelation was written around 96 AD in the midst of Roman rule. The Emperor Caesar Domitian had killed 40,000 Christians a few years before and the persecution of the church continued. But they are given this vision of Jesus—a Lion-Lamb King, ruling the world, coming back to make all things new.

Think about it: 2,000 years ago, Rome was the most powerful empire on earth. Jesus had twelve disciples and 120 followers. Now, 2,000 years later, Caesar is a salad, while two billion people claim to follow Christ, and many of them would die for his name. Why? Because Jesus is *worthy* (v 9).

This phrase "every tribe and language and people and nation" occurs four other times in Revelation. It's a big deal. All of these words are synonyms of each other; the aim isn't to parse out each meaning—they indicate the same thing. This is a point of emphasis, a literary tool that says, *literally every single color and culture under the sun shares in this redemption.*

Jesus has rescued a multi-ethnic bride. This new people of God is made up of Jews and Arabs and Africans and Greeks and Italians and Serbs and Icelanders and Koreans and Mexicans and Armenians... The Lamb has purchased a multicultural people to reign with him. This Jesus will end all wars and division and conflict and racism and tribalism. And what unites us? The worship of the Lamb! We will sing "a new song" together.

Do you realize how powerful it is when we all gather on a Sunday morning? As political conservatives and liberals, as black and white and brown, old and young, rich and poor—all worshiping one God, singing one song, in one Spirit, to the one who is worthy! God's mission is global. We worship him today in France, in Uganda, in Brazil, in Germany, in India, in underground churches in Iran, under threat of death in China. All of us singing, *You are worthy!*

The majority of Muslims are in the Middle East, the majority of Hindus are in India, the majority of Buddhists are in Asia, but Christians are almost equally split across North America, South America, Europe, and Africa. Jesus has ransomed people from every tribe and language and people and nation (v 9). This is the passage that sent William Carey, the father of modern-day missions, to India. *I know there are people there who Jesus died for... so I must go to them and tell them.* Jesus said he isn't coming back until all the nations are reached. We can try to figure out Revelation all we want, but until every people group hears the gospel, the work isn't done:

> *And this gospel of the kingdom will be proclaimed throughout the whole world as a testimony to all nations, and then the end will come. (Matthew 24:14)*

The word "nation" in the Bible doesn't refer to countries—countries change all the time. It's the Greek word *ethne* where we get our word "ethnicity." *Ethne* is a people group—a tribe, who share a common culture and a common language. There are 16,000 people groups on the planet, and 6,000 of them are unreached—which means they have no way of hearing about Jesus at all.

Over 2 billion people in the world today are classified as unreached.

And here's why it matters: Jesus is worthy to receive the praise of not just 10,000 people groups on the planet, but all 16,000 of them! He deserves to be worshiped in every language. Indeed, the promise of Philippians 2 is that one day every knee will bow and every tongue confess that Jesus Christ is Lord (v 10-11).

Lift your eyes, lift up your gaze, and see a global God doing a global thing. And then hear his invitation to join in.

GOD'S GLOBAL PLAN

Have you ever wondered why there are so many nations and languages? There are 195 countries in the world and 6,500 different languages. Why so many?

It feels like a good question to ask, because it seems as if the cause of many of our problems is in fact our differences. Maybe if we were one people, maybe if we had one ideology—the same philosophy, the same goal, the same laws and language and culture and ways of doing things—then maybe there wouldn't be wars. Maybe there wouldn't be the hate that divides us; maybe we could actually have peace on earth. What's interesting though, is that all throughout the Bible God scatters people. He's always sending.

First, he scatters the nations in judgment in Genesis 11, when they try to unite around one city, one tower, and one god: themselves. In Genesis 12, God calls Abraham to go without knowing where God is sending him (Hebrews 11:8) to become a nation that blesses every nation. And in Acts 1, before Jesus ascends into heaven, he tells the apostles to scatter from Jerusalem into the surrounding regions, even to the ends of the earth. As it turns out, they are scattered through persecution (see Acts 8).

God is always sending and scattering: "Now those who were scattered went about preaching the word" (Acts 8:4). The nations were scattered in judgment after Babel; now God wants his people scattered for salvation; he wants diversity and multiple cultures and many nations, colors and languages.

Remember, God's vision for the world is that his glory would fill the earth (Habakkuk 2:14). In every nation, every people, in every language, the glory of God made known! There is something about God—something about his beauty, about who he is, about the presence of God being in every place, that is far better, far more unifying, far more peacemaking than any sort of diplomacy or treaty or war could ever produce.

Michael Gorman comments on Revelation that "God's eschatological reality is ultimately about reconciliation among peoples—the 'healing of the nations' (Rev 22:2)—and not just individual salvation. This corporate reconciliation takes place when people from every tribe and tongue and nation center their lives on God and the

Lamb."[25] Like Revelation 5, a similar scene shows up in chapter 7:

After this I looked, and behold, a great multitude that no one could number, from every nation, from all tribes and peoples and languages, standing before the throne and before the Lamb, clothed in white robes, with palm branches in their hands, and crying out with a loud voice, "Salvation belongs to our God who sits on the throne, and to the Lamb!"

(Revelation 7:9-10)

These two multicultural vistas are meant, in part, to encourage us to look out at the people that are different from us—with different values, ideologies, philosophies—and to understand that Jesus is Lord over all the earth and King of all people, and that he has sent us to proclaim him as King.

Here's a question for your heart—read this slowly and make it a prayer: *what is keeping me from being involved in this mission?*

A global God offers a global solution to a global problem: a global gospel and a global church on a global mission. What might stop us being on board, going all-in with all we have, to be a part of that?

25 Michael J. Gorman, *Reading Revelation Responsibly: Uncivil Worship and Witness: Following the Lamb into the New Creation* (Cascade Books, 2011) p 218.

GLOBAL MISSIONS

I recently watched a fascinating documentary[26] on the church in Iran. It's an underground, secret church, because it's very dangerous to be a Christian there. Yet God is moving in amazing ways.

For example, a pastor in the documentary told a story about meeting a man in a small village who shared that, for the last couple of weeks, every night when he went to sleep, a man had appeared in his room and told him to write down everything that he said. When the pastor went to read his writings, he saw on the first page: *In the beginning was the Word, and the Word was with God and the Word was God...* Jesus was showing up in the middle of the night and dictating the Gospel of John to this ordinary Muslim man in an Iranian village! These stories are not as rare as you might think.[27]

But what struck me the most in the documentary was a story about the pastor's wife. He is American and she is Iranian. They had escaped religious oppression and persecution in Iran and come to America, where they could freely live out their faith. After living there a while, the wife pleaded with her husband to move back to Iran. "You're crazy," he told her. "You could be raped, beaten, or killed for your faith back there." But she insisted. Her

26 *Sheep Among Wolves*, https://www.youtube.com/watch?v=Ndf8RqgNVEY (accessed February 12, 2024).

27 https://www.thegospelcoalition.org/article/muslims-dream-jesus/ (accessed February 12, 2024).

argument? "The church here is under a satanic lullaby and I'm falling asleep."

They had experienced one of the most dangerous places to be a Christian, but the sleepy American church was a greater threat to her faith than the persecution in Iran.

How do we not fall asleep?

Well, we must lift our eyes, lift up our gaze, and see a global God doing a *global* thing. Intentional involvement is one way to stay awake.

William Carey once said that to know the will of God, we need an open Bible and an open map. Why? "For God is the King of all the earth … God reigns over the nations" (Psalm 47:7-8). Global mission is simply the proclamation of the coronation of a global King.

Here's how it works. Faith comes by hearing (Romans 10:17). But how can someone hear about Jesus unless someone preaches (v 14)? Sure, Jesus can speak directly to Iranian dreamers, but God wants us to play a part in his cosmic, global drama. And then who can preach "unless they are sent" (v 15)? So, there's someone in Iran (or wherever) who needs to hear about Jesus. There's someone who needs to go and preach. And there's someone who needs to send them. Which one are you?

SENDERS: PRAY. CARE. FUND

We can all champion the cause of a global King being made known to all his global elect. Just like a church-planting church needs a sending culture, a global-missions church needs a supportive community to *send* people out.

Senders pray: I once heard a story about a faithful missionary who served a particular region. One winter was especially harsh and he was unable to get to the village on the other side of the mountain. He was only able to serve the village on his side. But he would pray. Through tears he prayed for the people he couldn't reach. Spring came and the missionary was finally able to trek to the village he had labored in prayer for. What he found surprised him—they had spiritually grown far more than the village he could access. His labored prayers found favor with the global King. Senders can be spiritually and supernaturally effective even at a distance. Pray boldly—where both your heart and your faith are stretched.

Senders care: goers need the covering of a church family that pursues friendship and care all the more when they leave. Senders make sure there's no "out of sight, out of mind" mentality with the missionaries sent overseas. The further the goers go, the further the senders reach to love and care for them.

Senders fund: goers need money and resources from those with the regular income of ordinary jobs. Champion the cause of Christ to the nations financially, both individually and in community with your church. Give sacrificially—to the point it hurts.

GOERS: CALLED. EQUIPPED. SENT.

There are 54,056 evangelical Christians for every one unreached people group.[28] Either God is terrible at ratios or too many of us won't pause to listen to see if maybe we're called to go.

The goers are called: there's a spiritually discerned sense of the call of God to go. It's confirmed by your community and church (Acts 13:2). The context of biblical community and the covering of biblical authority will clarify your call and keep you safe.

The goers are equipped: you'll need a robust theology of the mission of God. Leadership training. Language training. Cross-cultural evangelism training. The church is not scarcely resourced—between the Spirit and the church, we've got you.

The goers are sent: there will be laying on of hands. There will be the grief of gospel goodbyes (see chapter 7). You'll be funded, supported, prayed over, and cared for by your community.

What is the reason that men and women would sell everything they have, move across the globe, and settle into the hard work of preaching the gospel to those in a different culture, with a different language and to many who worship a different god?

It's a vision: a Lamb who was slain for every tribe,

---

28 https://www.thetravelingteam.org/stats (accessed February 12, 2024).

language, people, and nation. He is worthy of all praise. This means we give our whole lives—our whole bodies even, as a living sacrifice to the Lord, even unto death. He is worthy!

A global God offers a global solution to a global problem: a global gospel and a global church on a global mission.

So, take a deep breath.

Consider.

Are you called to go?

ACTION STEPS

- Do you see yourself primarily as a sender or as a goer? How can you embrace both the sending and going parts of the Christian life? Which aspects of each role would you like to grow into?

- Does your church family have members who have moved from other countries? Invite a Christian of a different nationality to your home for a meal to get to know them and find out more about the church in their country.

- Do you know any missionaries who may need encouragement in their service for Jesus? Send a text, write an email, or mail them a letter to remind them that they are cared for.

5. A REDEMPTIVE PRESENCE

Seek the welfare of the city where I have sent you into exile, and pray to the LORD on its behalf, for in its welfare you will find your welfare.
Jeremiah 29:7

The woman sitting in front of me is in prison.

She is a former prostitute who has been through a program we sponsor at our church, and I would see her working as a server regularly at a restaurant near the church offices (really good burgers). She started coming on Sundays; her faith seemed genuine. But now I'm in this cold, hard place.

She got caught using drugs again and she won't get out for a good long while. This woman has made sinful, foolish choices in response to sinful, foolish things done to her, and it reminds me that I do the same thing. If all she needed was a second chance, if all she needed was some help, then she wouldn't be talking to me through plexiglass right now. I see this pattern in the prison of my own heart sometimes. What she needs is the same thing that you and I need today, again. Her only hope is the free and freeing truth of the gospel.

WHY ARE YOU HERE?

If you're questioning why you find yourself in a particular place at a particular time—prison visiting room or otherwise—you can know without doubt that when and where you are has been predetermined by the sovereign purpose and plan of God. *Where you are is where God sent you.*

In Acts 17, the apostle Paul isn't writing a book to church folk about their sent-ness, but the theological reality he cites is certainly relevant to this point. Hear this:

And he made from one man every nation of mankind to live on all the face of the earth, having determined allotted periods and the boundaries of their dwelling place, that they should seek God, and perhaps feel their way toward him and find him. (Acts 17:26-27)

Two helpful truths emerge. First, your neighbor to the right of you, as well as the one to your left, is not there by accident. God has orchestrated 10,000 things for them to be there, "that they should seek God" (v 27). Second, *where* you are and *when* you are there is also purposed by God. Thus, in fact, you are *sent* wherever you are.

Take this classic text in Jeremiah:

Thus says the LORD of hosts, the God of Israel, to all the exiles whom I have sent into exile from Jerusalem to Babylon: Build houses and live in them; plant gardens and eat their produce. Take wives and have sons and daughters; take wives for your sons, and give your daughters in marriage, that they may bear sons and daughters; multiply there, and do not decrease. But seek the welfare of the city where I have sent you into exile, and pray to the LORD on its behalf, for in its welfare you will find your welfare. (Jeremiah 29:4-7)

God's people are in exile in Babylon. They want to go back to Jerusalem but God has a purpose for them where they are—"I have sent [you] into exile" (v 4). *Buy a house. Cultivate the land. Start a business. Get married. Start families. You're going to be here for a while.* And "seek the welfare of the city" (v 7). Literally, the *shalom* of the city. Shalom means more than peace, it means human flourishing—wholeness.

Essentially, God is saying to them and to us that a part of our sent-ness is local. Christians are to live intentionally, missionally, and redemptively—being salt and light in the place where they are. And it's not just a message we bring but a manner of life. Not just words, but deeds too. So the question then is: what does it look like to be a redemptive presence in the place where God has already sent you?

RIGHT HAND, LEFT HAND

Here's the controversy, the conflict, the rub when talking about justice issues to an evangelical crowd. We're nervous about losing our evangelical witness to a bunch of soup-kitchen opportunities. Sent to the nations to preach? *Yes.* Sent to plant churches that proclaim the gospel? *I'm theologically in. But let's not become one of those social-gospel churches.* You needn't be concerned.

It's right hand and left hand: our ministry is word and deed working together. The word ministry—our proclamation and witness of who Jesus is and what Jesus has done—is the right hand. It's stronger (as a lefty, this illustration is offensive, though it is mine). It's most important. It's of first importance (1 Corinthians 15:3).

But we need lefties too. It is grace that saves, but grace is shown in acts of mercy, even if it means getting our hands dirty. People need Jesus, but they also need practical help sometimes. Jesus came preaching and teaching, but he also met tangible needs (Matthew 4:23). Jesus was ambidextrous, and we should be too.

In Acts 6, we see this right-and-left-hand ministry working hand in hand:

> *Now in these days when the disciples were increasing in number, a complaint by the Hellenists arose against the Hebrews because their widows were being neglected in the daily distribution. And the twelve summoned the full number of the disciples and said, "It is not right*

that we should give up preaching the word of God to serve tables. Therefore, brothers, pick out from among you seven men of good repute, full of the Spirit and of wisdom, whom we will appoint to this duty. But we will devote ourselves to prayer and to the ministry of the word." (Acts 6:1-4)

The church is growing, they are "increasing in number" (v 1)—things are going well. But there's a group in the church who aren't being cared for. The Hellenists start complaining that their widows are not being treated as fairly as the Hebrew widows. The Hellenists are the Greeks. They were probably, generations before, exiled during the Babylonian captivity. So culturally they are Greek, not Jewish. And sadly, because of their ethnicity and different culture, they were being overlooked. They were a minority of a minority of a minority—widows, women, and Gentiles.

The apostles, rightly, see this as an injustice. But notice their priorities. "It is not right that we should give up preaching the word of God to serve tables" (v 2). The church's priority is to minister the word—to teach and shepherd and counsel and pray and lead the people through the ministry of the gospel. In fact, the same word for "serve" in verse two—to *serve tables*—is the same word in verse four when they speak of the "*ministry of the word.*"

Here's my point: while it's vital that we prioritize the proclamation of the gospel and the ministry of the word, it's essential that we "adorn" the gospel (Titus 2:10) by our good deeds, as we seek the gospel renewal of our city.

THE PRESENCE OF THE CHURCH

A city on a hill. A royal priesthood. A holy nation. Salt and light. The very presence of a local church is redemptive.

Rodney Stark, the church historian, writes, "To cities filled with the homeless and impoverished, Christianity offered charity as well as hope. To cities filled with newcomers and strangers, orphans and widows, Christianity provided a new and expanded sense of family. To cities torn by ethnic strife, Christianity offered a new basis for social solidarity ... what [Christianity] brought was not simply an urban movement, but a new culture."[29]

The church is to be a redemptive presence: a counterculture in the midst of another one, an upside-down kingdom embedded in the kingdom of the world. We are the city of God inside the gates of the city of man. Like a Trojan horse of love and light, Jesus sends his church to the frontlines.

To say we are *redemptive* is to say that we *bring about change at a cost to ourselves*. This means it may cost us comfort, it may cost us social status; it will take time, energy, money, and relational equity, but love compels

---

29 Rodney Stark, *The Rise of Christianity: A Sociologist Reconsiders History* (Princeton University Press, 1996), p 161.

us to draw near to our neighbor for the sake of the gospel.

To say we are a *presence* is to say we are here, uniquely *in* the world but not *of* the world. In fact, Jesus prayed this very thing:

I have given them your word, and the world has hated them because they are not of the world, just as I am not of the world. I do not ask that you take them out of the world, but that you keep them from the evil one. They are not of the world, just as I am not of the world. Sanctify them in the truth; your word is truth. As you sent me into the world, so I have sent them into the world. (John 17:14-18)

How do we do this? How do we "seek the welfare of the city" where God has placed us as elect exiles? Consider three categories of redemptive presence: *intercession, faith and work,* and *justice.*

1. INTERCESSION

Jesus taught us intercessory prayer: "Your kingdom come, your will be done, on earth as it is in heaven" (Matthew 6:10). Intercession inhabits the space between heaven and earth; between what is and what should be; between God and man. It's a priestly function and we are made holy priests in Christ.

"Seek the welfare of the city where I have sent you into exile, *and pray to the LORD on its behalf*" (Jeremiah 29:7).

When we see something broken in the city, or something in a friend's life that doesn't line up with God's way, we pray, *Father, your kingdom come on earth as it is in heaven.* Intercession flows out of love for God and love for people. Richard Foster says, "If we truly love people, we will desire for them far more than it is within our power to give them, and this will lead us to prayer. Intercession is a way of loving others."[30]

Jesus is seeking intercessors for what's broken in your city. May it not be in vain: "And I sought for a man among them who should build up the wall and stand in the breach before me for the land, that I should not destroy it, *but I found none*" (Ezekiel 22:30).

Do you believe your prayers actually matter? In his book on prayer, Tyler Staton asks, "As a thought experiment, try to recall everything you've prayed for in the last week. If God answered every last one of your prayers, what would happen?"[31] Are your prayers so vague it would be hard to see if God answered them or not? *Seek the welfare of the city… and pray in faith!*

We don't know all the ways in which God answers our prayers, but he invites us into this ministry of intercession for our cities. Look around you—labor in prayer for the things that burden your heart!

---

30 Richard Foster, *Prayer: Finding the Heart's True Home* (HarperCollins, 1992), p 191.

31 Tyler Staton, *Living Like Monks, Praying like Fools* (Zondervan, 2022), p 96.

2. FAITH AND WORK

My church is in the city center and our members inhabit every sphere of influence—government, education, business, the arts, medicine, media—as a redemptive presence. They spend an hour or so at church on a Sunday and a couple of hours a week in biblical community, but what about the other 164 hours in their week?

Martin Luther famously said, "God doesn't need your work, but your neighbor does."[32] So Christian teachers are serving their neighbors and showing the city how Jesus would teach a class. Christian lawyers are serving their neighbors and showing how Jesus would write a just contract. Christian chefs serve their neighbors and show how Jesus would make a meal. Christian politicians serve their neighbors and show how Jesus would govern a city.[33]

Tim Keller offers four considerations for how our faith intersects with our work and how that brings a little salt and light to the city where we dwell:

First, the Christian faith gives us a moral compass, an inner GPS giving us ethical guidance that takes us beyond merely the legal aspects or requirements in any situation.

Second, your Christian faith gives you a new spiritual power, an inner gyroscope, that keeps you from being

---

32 Gustaf Wingren, *Luther on Vocation* (Wipf and Stock, 2004), p 10.

33 In a concert of Christian diversity, I am grateful for Gene Vieth, Tim Keller, and Tony Evans for helping me form these ideas.

overthrown by either success, failure, or boredom. Regarding success and failure, the gospel helps Christians find their deepest identity not in our accomplishments but who we are in Christ.

Third, the Christian faith gives us a new conception of work as the means by which God loves and cares for his world through us. Look at the places in the Bible that say that God gives every person their food. How does God do that? It is through human work.

Fourth, the Christian faith gives us a new world-and-life view that shapes the character of our work. All well-done work that serves the good of human beings pleases God.[34]

So much of our lives orients around our vocation; shouldn't so much of our ministry intersect with our work? Our redemptive presence begs the question, *how does the gospel work itself out in my work?*

3. JUSTICE

I heard Paul Miller once say, "Love begins with looking." In a similar way, I think justice begins with listening:

O LORD, you hear the desire of the afflicted; you will strengthen their heart; you will incline your ear to do justice to the fatherless and the oppressed, so that man who is of the earth may strike terror no more.

(Psalm 10:17-18)

---

34 https://timothykeller.com/blog/2014/3/7/how-faith-affects-our-work (accessed February 12, 2024).

Over and again, the prophets in the Old Testament confront God's people with their lack of justice. They won't listen. Jesus' brother James warns us of the same thing in the New Testament: "Behold, the wages of the laborers who mowed your fields, which you kept back by fraud, are crying out against you, and the cries of the harvesters have reached the ears of the Lord of hosts" (James 5:4).

So first start with listening. What are the cries of your city? What can the church do that the city can't? Maybe the homeless need to be fed, but maybe your city (like mine) already has programs for them. Maybe those people just need relationship, empowerment, and dignity. What's the racial climate in your city? Is there a community of refugees? What about their kids? Practicing justice may mean getting out of your comfort zone to incline your ear to the cries of the oppressed in your city.

My friend Melissa started a non-profit that builds relationships with women who are caught up in the sex industry. She gave me some advice to share for how to get going. But you don't always have to be the one to start something; there could be some great work already happening where you are—jump in! Here are her tips:

- Start somewhere! Like finding a new sport or hobby, you might have to try a few before you land on the right one, but you have to start somewhere.

- Don't defer responsibility or assume that there is a group of zealous Christians with tons of margin and they've got it covered—they are just ordinary people motivated by Scripture with lots of responsibilities and full lives—they need your help!

- Dream of what the church could do for the world if everyone pitched in—what kind of testimony would that be to a hurting, broken, and angry world whose Lord is "self"?

BE PRESENT

I wonder if we're often paralyzed into passivity, not exactly sure what to do first or next, when possibly only our presence is required. I've learned that both as a pastor and parent. My presence is what brings people comfort in their suffering, more than finding the perfect words. My presence with my kids is what makes them feel safe and loved, not trying for perfect discipline or perfect fun! Isn't it in the presence of God himself where we find comfort?

The gospel is the great news that Jesus entered our neighborhood, walked our streets, cried our tears, and brought hope and healing through his life, death, and resurrection. Pursuing the gospel renewal of the city means we have to leave our safe church bubbles.

You are where you are because God has sent you. Don't wait for a perfect plan, don't think you need more preparation—start with being intentionally present, remembering your sent-ness, right here, right now. Trust the Spirit to lead you. Intercede on behalf of the city. And watch your heart begin to warm to your neighborhood and to its citizens—especially those most forgotten.

Your redemptive presence brings salt and light. That's what your city or town or village needs. And you'll find you need it too.

In its welfare you will find your welfare.

(Jeremiah 29:7)

ACTION STEPS

- Consider your different neighbors and make a list of them all (not just the people who live next-door but your coworker at the next desk; another parent in your child's class etc.) Prayerfully look out for opportunities to be a loving gospel presence in their lives.

- Do you have an understanding of why God has placed you in this specific place at this specific time? If you feel confused, pray for a revelation of his purposes and opportunities for you right now, however big or small they may seem.

- Which areas of need in your community break your heart or stir your passion the most? Research local mercy ministries where you could get involved. If you can't find any that fit the bill, perhaps you could speak to other church members or leaders about how your church may be able to serve your community and help to heal these areas of brokenness with the gospel.

6. FINDING *YOUR* PLACE

While they were worshiping the Lord and fasting, the Holy Spirit said, "Set apart for me Barnabas and Saul for the work to which I have called them." Then after fasting and praying they laid their hands on them and sent them off.

Acts 13:2-3

The mission of God disrupts our lives. He wants us to be on the front lines so we see what Jesus can do. But how do we discern our role?

The Pearsons just planted a church in New Mexico. Before that, they were part of a church-planting team in Portugal. Before that, they were deacons of missions at my church in Texas, sending missionaries and mission teams internationally. How did they discern God's call each time?

Leo planted a church in Brazil, where he grew up. Then God sent him and his family to Fort Worth, Texas to start a business. He plays guitar on our worship team and attends a small group. He's on mission in a culture that still doesn't quite understand how smart and funny he is, or how gifted.

I was a baseball player with no seminary degree and no college degree from Detroit, Michigan, sent to start a church in the South.

Peter the Rock was a quick-tempered fisherman.

Simon the Zealot was zealous for the wrong things.

Matthew collected taxes and then some...

There doesn't appear to be much rhyme or reason in Jesus' recruiting tactics. His strategy seems strange to say the least. So how do we find our place? What part do we play? Let me offer three things to meditate on as you prayerfully consider your role right now, and maybe a future role God has for you. Let's think about *providence, spiritual gifts,* and *calling.*

PROVIDENCE

The Heidelberg Catechism states:

What is the providence of God?

It is the almighty and everywhere present power of God, whereby, as it were, by his hand, he still upholds heaven and earth, with all creatures, and so governs them that herbs and grass, rain and drought, fruitful and barren years, meat and drink, health and sickness, riches and poverty, yea, all things come not by chance, but by his fatherly hand.[35]

---

35 Heidelberg Catechism (Question 27).

The word "providence" literally means "see to." God sees to everything; he makes it happen; he's got it. God sees what you can't see, and what God sees, he sees to. God will provide whatever is needed to see to it that his plans and purposes are accomplished. And how does he do that? He says it:

So shall my word be that goes out from my mouth;
  it shall not return to me empty,
but it shall accomplish that which I purpose,
  and shall succeed in the thing for which I sent it.
                                   (Isaiah 55:11)

God speaks and it's done; God decrees and it happens. And so, the question for us is this: how can we *hear* what God *sees*? If God is summoning a symphony of grace in your life right now, if he's orchestrating all things for your good and his glory—how do we discern the music? What does it say?

Everything that happens, happens in the providence of God and according to his purpose. So we can "hear" his voice in every circumstance, and trust his guidance.

Remember Joseph? Big dreamer, Daddy's favorite, cool jacket. His brothers sell him into slavery, he ends up in jail, but God is with him, and he ends up basically ruling Egypt next to Pharaoh. His brothers come to get food during a famine and Joseph reveals himself to them after all these years. He says:

As for you, you meant evil against me, but God meant it

> for good, **to bring it about** that many people should be
> kept alive, as they are today. (Genesis 50:20)

To bring it about. To see to. His brothers meant to do evil—
their choices were meaningful, but even their evil falls
under the providence of God. Even through suffering and
evil, God is speaking and carrying out his plan.

God's providence also works out geographically, in
placing us where we're meant to be. In Acts 17, the
apostle Paul is in Athens, and they invite him to speak
at the Areopagus. Athens was the intellectual center of
the world—it's where Socrates and Plato and Aristotle
had birthed Greek philosophy and thought. And the
Areopagus was *the* place to discuss philosophical matters.
Paul is talking to a bunch of atheists and agnostics and
nonbelievers and he doesn't start by explaining the Bible,
he starts by explaining providence:

> And he made from one man every nation of mankind
> to live on all the face of the earth, having determined
> allotted periods and the boundaries of their dwelling
> place, that they should seek God, and perhaps feel their
> way toward him and find him. Yet he is actually not far
> from each one of us. (Acts 17:26-27)

Having determined allotted periods—when—*and the
boundaries of their dwelling place*—where—*that they
should seek God*—purpose.

Maybe you're thinking of moving, taking a new job,
planting a church, or being a missionary. I'm not sure

what God's will is for you in that decision, but I do know you are wherever you are right now because it's his will you would be there. Right now is not an accident and he's speaking to you in it. One author has said, "Christians gripped by providence have built hospitals, ended slave trades, founded orphanages, launched reformations, and pierced the darkness of unreached peoples."[36]

Providence provides the context in which Scripture and the wisdom of the Spirit are applied—but we still make meaningful choices. The popular saying "When God closes a door, he opens a window," turns providence into a formula. But an open door doesn't necessarily mean God wants us to walk through it. It may be a great opportunity, but the timing may not be right; it may be an opportunity for you to pray and think and talk with your community and find out that what you're doing right now is exactly where God has you. Maybe he will use the open door to actually galvanize your calling to stay. On the other hand, a closed door might mean he wants us to keep knocking, to keep praying, to keep asking.

It can feel a bit overwhelming to consider all the options, but people and prayer are your best friends when discerning God's providence. Ask your church and ask God which doors are closed for good and which ones still need to be knocked on.

---

36 https://www.desiringgod.org/articles/walk-in-his-providence (accessed February 12, 2024).

SPIRITUAL GIFTS

Spiritual gifts are the concrete, tangible manifestations of divine energy in and through followers of Jesus. The gifts are God himself working in and through us—God going "public" among his people.[37]

Every Christian is given at least one gift to participate in the discipleship and building up of the body (1 Corinthians 12:7). It is God the Holy Spirit who determines the gift(s) you receive (v 11) and each gift is necessary for the maturity of the church (v 14-26). Most importantly, the exercise and operation of the gifts must be done in love (chapter 13).

Realizing what gift(s) you have doesn't always give you a crystal-clear picture of finding your place in God's mission, but it does help a lot. For example, if you have the gift of *giving* (Romans 12:8), there's a good chance you're supposed to help underwrite God's sending of church plants, missionaries, and those engaging the city through non-profits and other types of service.

How do you know if you have the gift of *giving?*

1. Do you tend to see the needs of others more easily than other people you know?

2. Do you enjoy giving your time, talent, and treasure to others?

---

37 Sam Storms, *Practicing the Power* (Zondervan, 2017), p 15.

3. Do you see giving to a worthwhile project as an exciting honor and privilege?

4. When you give money to someone, do you find that you did not expect any appreciation in return?

5. Do you sense a great deal of joy in giving?

6. Do you find yourself looking for opportunities to give your money in response to needs?

Maybe you have the gift of *exhortation* or encouragement (v 8). Exhortation involves motivating, encouraging, and consoling others. It's the capacity to urge people to action in applying biblical truths—you're a spiritual cheerleader. If you have this gift, you might be a *sender* to someone's going. You may be a mobilizer in the local church that encourages people to God's mission.

Look hard enough, and you'll find an exhorter close to those whom God used greatly as leaders. The great Reformer Martin Luther sought to purify the church, and in doing so faced continual opposition and controversies. His life was in constant danger; many of his friends rejected and opposed him. As a result, Luther struggled mightily with deep depression. His wife, Katherine, was a gifted encourager who strengthened, supported, and counseled her husband as he spearheaded the Reformation. Without her gift of exhortation, it is doubtful whether Luther would have had the strength and will to continue pressing forward with his calling from God.[38]

How do you know if you have the gift of *exhortation?*

1. Do people seek you out for advice and encouragement?

2. Do you enjoy walking with someone through difficulties?

3. Are you attracted to those who are hurting and needy?

4. Do you enjoy working closely with people who have personal and emotional problems?

5. Would you rather speak personally with someone about their problems rather than send them to someone else for help?

6. Do you find it easy to bring joy to those who are suffering?

However, if you have the gift of *leadership* (v 8), your place could be to *start* the church or start the non-profit in the city. The spiritual gift of leadership is found in people who have a clear, significant vision and are able to communicate it, publicly or privately, in such a way that they help others to catch the vision and pursue it.

If you have a biblical vision for something—a hope for a

---

38 This example was taken from a PDF authored by Mark Driscoll on spiritual gifts.

better future—*and* you can inspire people to it, *and then* they actually follow you, that's the gift of leadership.

How do you know if you have the gift of *leadership?*

1. Do others have confidence in your ability to lead?

2. When a difficult situation arises, do others look to you for input and leadership?

3. Do you usually take leadership in a group where none exists?

4. Do others look to you to make the major decisions for a group or organization?

Here's one more: the gift of *administration* (1 Corinthians 12:28) is the God-given ability to give direction and to make decisions that result in efficient operation and accomplishment of goals. Often, the mark of an administrator is the ability to accomplish things in a "fitting and orderly way" (14:40, NIV). The Greek word conveys the idea of steering a ship or governing an organization.

Administrators often have a keen eye for detail and an intuitive understanding of how something needs to be accomplished. If this is your gift, you will be paramount in organizing *how* people are sent; whether through justice ministries, evangelism, or other missions efforts in your local church.

How do you know if you have the gift of *administration?*

1. Do you find it easy to make decisions?

2. When you give advice to someone, is your emphasis more about "how" it should be done than "why"?

3. Do you find yourself frequently thinking of decisions that need to be made to give overall direction to a group or organization?

4. Are you organized and efficient?

DISCERNING YOUR GIFT

Whatever your gift is, knowing that you have it can give you an insight into finding your place within God's mission. Think about this:

Where do you tend to feel frustrated in church?

Typically (and perhaps ironically!), this is where you tend to be spiritually gifted. Are you always saying or thinking, "This class could have been so much better if they had communicated it this way, signed people up like this and put the chairs here"—you might have the gift of administration. Or, "The church doesn't care enough for those in need; I wish we did more"—the gift of mercy!

In which ministry moments do you often find yourself?

Are you frequently praying for people? Maybe you have the gift of encouragement or mercy or faith. Are you always around non-Christians having meaningful conversations? Maybe you have the gift of evangelism (Ephesians 4:11).

What can you see yourself doing with joy over the long haul?

What kind of ministry is most life-giving to you?

Where are you most effective in ministry?

Every Christian can do (and is called to do) all of the gifts! Giving, serving, showing mercy, evangelizing... But you know it's a spiritual gift when you find both joy *and* effectiveness in it—even as you still grow in the gift and fan it into flame.

What does your community affirm in you?

Sometimes the best indicator of where your place is in God's mission is what your biblical community encourages in you. What kind of ministry do they seek from you? What do they see in you?

CALLING

The idea of "calling" can certainly be overstated (and also understated) depending on who you ask. Most pastors or theologians would affirm a biblical call to the family, the church, and the state—to prioritize family, to serve in community, and to be a good citizen. You are, at a minimum, *sent* by God in those three realms.

But we're asking the question, "Where do I find my place in God's mission?" And discerning a sense of call is more than just providence and our particular spiritual gifts—it's not just pure thought and logic, there seems to be a spiritual sense too. In fact, as we saw in the examples at the beginning of the chapter, sometimes God's calling doesn't seem logical! Pastor and author Darrell Johnson says, "He is always calling the church into mission beyond our resources so that we have to depend on him."[39]

> Now there were in the church at Antioch prophets and teachers, Barnabas, Simeon who was called Niger, Lucius of Cyrene, Manaen a lifelong friend of Herod the tetrarch, and Saul. While they were worshiping the Lord and fasting, the Holy Spirit said, "Set apart for me Barnabas and Saul for the work to which I have called them." Then after fasting and praying they laid their hands on them and sent them off. (Acts 13:1-3)

Notice that first "they were worshiping the Lord and fasting" (v 2). God can do anything—and I would never want to put him into some theological box—but he seems to desire our seeking, and sometimes it seems that's a prerequisite to him moving in a particular way. The leadership team at First Church Antioch sought the Lord for direction, and then they heard the Spirit say, "Set apart for me Barnabas and Saul for the work to which I have *called* them." It's the Spirit that calls us. It's through the Spirit that we can discern spiritual things (1 Corinthians 2:6-16).

39 Darrell W. Johnson, *Discipleship On The Edge: An Expository Journey Through the Book of Revelation* (Canadian Church Leaders Network, 2021), p. 110.

But then notice that it wasn't until "after fasting and praying" (v 3) again that they send them to plant churches. They had a sense of call, they heard the Spirit, but they still sought confirmation in community.

So what is your calling? Ask God to help you and ask yourself these questions:

Am I being faithful to my calling to my family, my church, and my city?

Even if you sense a call to expanded ministry, you won't be ready yet until you are faithful with what God has called you to first.

Through Scripture, providence, prayer, and the Spirit, what does it seem God is calling me to?

If you think God is calling you to something Scripture explicitly forbids, you obviously haven't heard him right!

Does my family and community agree?

The people that know you best can discern with you best.

Do my church leaders affirm my call?

Let your pastors encourage and, yes, even challenge you.

What are my spiritual gifts?

The Spirit sovereignly gave you specific gifts; embrace them, don't despise them.

However you wrestle with finding your place, know this: you have a place!

As a pastor, I love seeing passion and drive in people. I would much rather have to redirect some misplaced or immature zeal than to have to stir it up in the first place. The clarity of your call might slowly materialize, like wiper blades washing a dusty car window. Or maybe it will happen quickly, like a lightning bolt. Either way, the important thing is to know that *you* have been sent *by* God for the *mission* of God and the glory of his name.

ACTION STEPS

- Can you think of an example from your life where you became aware of God's providence, or when wise Christian friends helped you to see how he was working?

- Do you have an understanding of the spiritual gifts you've been given? Work through some of the questions listed in this chapter to see which gifts you can identify in yourself. Speak to friends or leaders from your church to help you gain a wider perspective on what your gifting might be.

- When have you felt called by God in the past? How about for the future?

7. GOSPEL GOODBYES

And there was much weeping on the part of all; they embraced Paul and kissed him, being sorrowful most of all because of the word he had spoken, that they would not see his face again.

Acts 20:37-38

I ordered the Meat Burger (two patties, cheese, egg, avocado, topped with brisket). Ryan ordered a chicken sandwich—we're pretty different. Today was our monthly lunch: friendship, partnership, fellowship.

Twelve years ago, Ryan was serving faithfully in my church. He started leading, eventually came on staff and later became a pastor. Then he caught a vision and a calling to plant a church down the road—not too far away, but far enough that we wouldn't be able to play nerf basketball in the office anymore.

The gospel sends us because people meeting Jesus is more important than our comforts. We can't stay cozy and cosseted, keeping everyone we love close by—sometimes we have to say goodbye. It's a gospel goodbye; there's a joy to it, but also a sorrow. We're glad, because we know that God is sending people out for his glory; but we grieve also. Gospel goodbyes happen when your relationships have their foundation in God's overarching story.

GOODBYE, EPHESUS

In Acts 20, we get a profound insight into the relational ministry that the apostle Paul had with many of his fellow ministers, at least in Ephesus. Paul spent three years in Ephesus and then traveled to the surrounding cities encouraging other churches. He was on his way to Jerusalem when he stopped in Miletus and called for the pastors at Ephesus to meet with him about 30 miles away (v 17).

God did amazing things through Paul and this church in Ephesus—they experienced so much together (which you can read about in Acts 19). This was a church so open about their lives together that it was normal for them to confess their sins to one another. A bunch of them had been into dark arts and magic and when they became Christians, they came together and burned all their books (v 19).

Paul left right after a city riot that took place because so many people were now worshiping Jesus as God that no one was buying the little idols of the god Artemis anymore. This church in Ephesus had grown in influence to the point that it affected the economic culture of the city as Jesus transformed his people. Here's the point: Paul and the Ephesian elders shared incredible gospel stories!

And when he had said these things, he knelt down and prayed with them all. And there was much weeping on the part of all; they embraced Paul and kissed him, being sorrowful most of all because of the word he had spoken, that they would not see his face again. And they accompanied him to the ship. (Acts 20:36-38)

This is an emotional moment. Paul had spent quality time with them—they had broken bread together, laughed together, and cried together. They had inside jokes and funny memories. They went through painful experiences in ministry together. They had conflict and had to forgive and reconcile. They spent three years planting this church together, witnessing people being redeemed and restored by Jesus—it was a lot of history! So many gospel stories—and now a gospel goodbye.

In our twelve years as a church we have sent out hundreds of college seniors, multiplied scores of small groups, and sent out eight elders and 250 people to plant four churches. We've served with them, shared meals with them, heard their stories, baptized them, cried with them through marriage struggles; our kids have played with their kids. And we've worshiped together—there's something that binds people together when they sing; when they eat the bread and drink the wine together week in and week out.

Ryan and I experienced a lot with each other. Besides nerf basketball dunk competitions in the office, we also traveled together. We went to Seattle for a church conference and told an NHL hockey referee about Jesus on the plane. We went with our wives to the beach in Florida, and shared the backstory of our lives—the real stuff, the dark and light events of our stories that really make up who someone is. But most of our experiences together were in the everyday, mundane, ordinary parts of life and ministry. We shared in the hardships and joys of gospel ministry—the celebrations of God's work in our people and the grieving of sin's work in our people.

It was the same for Paul and the Ephesian leaders: "You yourselves know how I lived among you the whole time from the first day that I set foot in Asia ... teaching you in public and from house to house" (Acts 20:18, 20). He didn't just share the gospel but also his life.

It's a great example and definition of discipleship: we share the gospel *and* our lives with each other. When Paul left the Ephesians, they didn't just lose a pastor, they lost a friend.

Gospel goodbyes don't really happen if you don't live life *with* people. If you're too emotionally guarded with people and don't take risks, you won't really be known, so when you leave, it won't be a *gospel* goodbye—just a goodbye.

Oftentimes a gospel goodbye feels like taking a huge risk. Paul said, "I am going to Jerusalem, constrained by the

Spirit, not knowing what will happen to me there, except that the Holy Spirit testifies to me in every city that imprisonment and afflictions await me" (Acts 20:22-23). Paul knows that going to Jerusalem is a risk. Living a sent life is scary sometimes.

That looks like the Pearson family, who left their community and friends and went to Portugal to plant a church in a place vastly different than their culture and knowing no one. Or like a small group that multiplies—you already know these people, it's comfortable, and creating two new groups is like starting over. What if it doesn't work? Or like people leaving a church they love to start a new one. I want to acknowledge that as you consider your sent-ness, it's a relational risk. It's an emotional moment. Ministry isn't only programs and events and churches and mission trips—it's real community, and it sometimes means leaving that community you have invested so much in.

I love how human the Bible is; the writer of Acts says that when Paul left the Ephesian church members "there was much weeping" (v 37). They're grieving, and of course they are. The friendship itself isn't ending; all of us have that friend that we could be away from for years and then see each other and pick right back up from where we left off. So what they're grieving is the loss of proximity—they're grieving the sharing of their lives.

Proximity is so important in relationships. Your energy and love and focus and time in relationships probably

Jim Essian

should be directed to those God has put you around—those God has sent you to. And so, when he calls them (or you) away obviously the relationship has to change.

HOW TO SAY GOODBYE

If we live on mission and go to a sending church, gospel goodbyes will be normal. Groups multiply, churches are planted, missionaries leave, students graduate. Our relationships will change; proximity becomes approximation; every day or every week becomes every once in a while. How do we prepare our hearts and shepherd one another's souls, without keeping everyone at arm's length for fear of finally finding community, only to leave, or see them go?

1. IT'S BETTER TO GRIEVE THAN TO IGNORE

Grief needs acknowledgement or it becomes too powerful; it's an emotion not an identity. Address the loss. You can be a Christian and still be sad. Your faith isn't failing when you're not happy—in fact, your faith is full when you grieve before the face of God. I love what pastor and author Zack Eswine says: "In this fallen world, sadness is an act of sanity, our tears the testimony of the sane."[40]

I have learned with my kids that getting them to acknowledge and talk through a moment of suffering—

---

40 Zack Eswine, *Spurgeon's Sorrows: Realistic Hope for those who Suffer from Depression* (Christian Focus, 2015) p 19.

like falling off their bike—helps their brains to process what happened. It frames a story around the sad event that actually took place, instead of a more fearful tale developing later. Apparently, this is backed by neurology.[41] So grieve. And encourage others to grieve by asking good questions:

- What will you miss the most about them leaving?

- What fears do you have around their absence?

- What do you think will change?

2. IT'S HARDER TO LEAVE THAN TO BE LEFT

For the most part, it will be harder for the new group that's multiplying, or the church planter (and team) leaving, or the missionary going than those staying back. Those leaving are starting something new. It's unknown; it's uncomfortable. It's exciting, yes, but different, vulnerable, scary, and probably a little lonely.

Those that stay grieve those who leave but they still have what's known and comfortable. It's easy for those who leave to feel forgotten—out of sight, out of mind. My counsel? The ones who are left might consider taking the initiative to intentionally reach out. Set calendar reminders. Pray for them. Let them know you miss them. Send cards, gifts, texts.

---

41 See Daniel J. Siegel, Tina Payne Bryson, *The Whole-Brain Child* (Random House, 2012).

If your small group multiplies, consider bringing both groups together once a quarter and celebrate all God is doing as an extended family. If your friends go to help plant a church, visit on a Sunday if possible a couple of times a year. Be creative in your support!

3. IT'S EASIER TO SUBMIT TO SEASONS THAN TO LIVE IN THE PAST

Ecclesiastes 3 is famous for its comforting wisdom: there's a time for everything, and for everything there's a season. "A time to keep, and a time to cast away" (v 6). Relationships change—Christians overuse phrases like, *this season has been so hard,* but, clichés aside, submitting to whatever season God has for you is better than not.

Things change, but God is sovereign over it all. Trust he has new adventures, new relationships, new ministries for you. Staying in the past is certainly more comfortable, but what God is doing right now is an invitation to grow. I heard a counselor once say, "Stay at the edge of your growth and invite the Spirit there." God's not done with you yet!

GOODBYE, FOR NOW

Gospel goodbyes are sad, but there's a glory to them. We know the goodbye is good: the mission advances, the knowledge of God's glory grows, Christ's name is exalted. Our joyful sorrow is part of our witness. So often, the world experiences people separating and leaving through division and strife and irreconcilable differences and church splits. Gospel goodbyes show the world something different.

The world divides, the church sends. The world separates, the church multiplies.

As Christians, we believe in an eternal community, a kingdom that cannot be shaken, a forever Bride. Gospel goodbyes, then, are never final.

On the night of his arrest, Jesus grieved his friends with the plain words of his subsequent departure. He spoke of it often (Luke 13:33; Matthew 16:21; Matthew 17:22; Mark 8:31), but the disciples just never got it. This time they did: "Because I have said these things to you, sorrow has filled your heart" (John 16:6).

But the sorrow won't last forever. Our hope is for that glorious vision of all God's people worshiping him as one; reunited in body and soul. Goodbyes are not forever; our sorrow is only temporary. As Jesus said, "You have sorrow now, but I will see you again, and your hearts will rejoice" (v 22).

ACTION STEPS

- Can you recall any gospel goodbyes that you've experienced over the years? Could you send a message of support or comfort to someone in your church who may be grieving the departure of a friend that has been called to a new location?

- Can you plan to visit and encourage former church friends who have left to serve God elsewhere?

- Or do you need to welcome any brothers and sisters who are new to your church or new to serving in a ministry team?

8. DREAM BIG

*Now to him who is able to do far more abundantly than
all that we ask or think, according to the power at work
within us, to him be glory in the church and in Christ
Jesus throughout all generations.*
Ephesians 3:20-21

When I was preparing to plant my church, I didn't know what I was doing. I had no seminary degree, no college degree, no formal training—so I read a ton of books and found a pastor by the name of Martyn Lloyd-Jones to be a relevant help. He was dead already, so he wasn't exactly a mentor, but his books and sermons had a profound impact on me.

Lloyd-Jones pastored in urban London in the mid-1900s as England began to head towards the post-Christian culture it is now, much like my city is swiftly moving towards. The church in London was in decline, but his strategy was to unapologetically and expositionally preach through books of the Bible for 45 minutes—year after year, decade after decade, and people flocked to his church like hungry sheep looking for a shepherd to feed them.

He was the first to teach me about revival. I'd never really heard that word before, and certainly didn't understand it, but I wanted it. Lloyd-Jones grew up in Wales right after the huge Welsh revivals in the late 1800s and early 1900s, and he always prayed that God would do the same thing in his day and in his city. He never saw it, but he definitely prayed for it.

A revival isn't when a church sets up a tent outside and brings in a famous preacher hoping non-believers come. I actually saw a church in our city do that recently; they organized an event and called it Revival Night.

You can't plan a revival.

A revival is when the Spirit sovereignly shows up to awaken Christians already in the church. Richard Lovelace says, "A revival is an outpouring of the Holy Spirit which restores the people of God to normal spiritual life."[42] It's not produced, it's not frantic, it's not dramatic; it's the Spirit of God poured out on the people of God in a way that rouses them for the glory of God.

Here's my question though: would you be ready if God brought revival to your town?

---

42 Richard F. Lovelace, *Dynamics of Spiritual Life* (InterVarsity Press, 2020), p 40.

In his book, *A God-Sized Vision,* Collin Hansen writes about some of the historic revivals. But first he comments, "We submit that many Christians have grown so content with the ordinary that they don't bother asking God for anything more ... *Few of us are tempted today to dream too big* [emphasis mine]."[43]

DREAMS FOR THE FUTURE

Our dreams as a society have been quite affected in recent years, so say the scientists and sociologists.[44] There was a particular increase in dreams of a far more anxious and fearful nature than normal during the pandemic. Our sleep patterns changed—we slept a little longer, alongside a marked increase in alcohol and drug consumption, and it altered how we dream in a big way.

I wonder, however, if the anxiety of recent years revealed a desire for something more than what a stable, steady, successful existence can offer us. A desire for a movement of God, or to be used by God in a mighty way—to be caught up in something bigger than ourselves.

Few of us are tempted today to dream too big.

When you lie in bed at night, when all is quiet for a moment and you've slowed down enough to get below

---

43 Collin Hansen and John D. Woodbridge, *A God-Sized Vision* (Zondervan, 2015), p 12.

44 See https://thesleepdoctor.com/covid-19-and-sleep/covid-dreams/ and https://www.ncbi.nlm.nih.gov/pmc/articles/PMC8800372/#:~:text=Our%20work%20shows%20strong%20associations,activity%20and%20quality%20of%20life (accessed February 12, 2024).

the surface of your heart—what is it you're really after? What are you pursuing? What do you dream of?

Seriously, take a moment and ask your heart that question: *what do I dream of for my life and ministry?*

We need prophetic imagination.
We need kingdom visionaries.
We need missional dreamers.

Don't forget, we are children of the King who fear nothing and no man, for the glory of God and the good of all people. What if we took some risks and dreamed some big dreams?

If dreaming big feels like something you just can't connect with, if you feel distant from God and his plans and purposes for your life, the book of Hosea offers some advice: "Break up your fallow ground, for it is time to seek the LORD, that he may come and rain righteousness upon you" (10:12). This verse comes near the end of the book, which as a whole is basically a living parable of God's faithful love for a faithless people. It's a pretty bleak story, but full of redemptive grace and mercy. God calls Israel to return to him and he will revive them. They have "plowed iniquity" (v 13) and therefore will reap "injustice" (v 13). But if they "sow … righteousness" they will reap "steadfast love" (v 12). In fact, all they have to do is repent and turn back to God, and God himself will "rain righteousness" on them. In his sermon on this verse, A.W. Tozer writes:

*Miracles follow the plow ... In every denomination,
missionary society, local church or individual Christian,
this law operates. God works as long as His people live
daringly ... The power of God comes only where it is
called out by the plow. It is released into the Church
only when she is doing something that demands it.*[45]

Maybe it's time to plow deep into the ground of your
relationship with Jesus, and begin to dream big dreams
for how God might use you.

A DREAM-BIG PRAYER

In Ephesians 3, the apostle Paul is praying for the
Ephesian church, and his prayer is for us too. We see
two themes emerge as he prays, and the first is for
strength: "He may grant you to be strengthened with
power through his Spirit in your inner being" (v 16). He's
saying, *Deep in your very being, I want you to be strong in
the Spirit.*

Then in verse 18, he prays that we would "have strength
to comprehend" with the whole church, the fullness of
God's love. The world is in opposition to the kingdom
of God, and it's fighting to pull you away, to lure you
back into its kingdom. You need strength, endurance
and steadfastness to increase in your knowledge and
everyday experience of the love of God. So, the second
theme is God's *love.* In verse 17, he prays that we would

---

45 A.W. Tozer sermon, "Miracles that Follow the Plow"

be "rooted and grounded in love," and in verse 19, that we would "know the love of God that surpasses knowledge." Paul wants you to experience God's love, not just know that it exists. We need spiritual strength to increase our experiential knowledge of God's love.

I listen to the Huberman Lab podcast, and one episode discussed the science of muscle growth. For a muscle to get stronger, it has to be stressed; there has to be weight, tension, exertion. Likewise, our spiritual heart—our spiritual strength—needs the same thing. God wants to stretch our faith, he wants us to seek him, to *live daringly,* to put our hands to the plow. Paul is essentially saying that our spiritual strength needs to grow to receive all that God is doing—to be filled with all the fullness of God. Jesus is ready to call you into something more than you can even ask or think or imagine, but maybe you're not ready yet to receive it.

There's a prayer from the *Valley of Vision* (a collection of Puritan prayers) that says, "There is still so much unconquered territory in my heart."[46] Are there corners of your heart that are not given over to him? The book, *Why Revival Tarries,* asks something similar: "Can the Holy Spirit be invited to take us by the hand down the corridors of our souls? Are there not secret springs, and secret motives that control, and secret chambers where other

---

46 Arthur G. Bennett, "A Minister's Praises" in *The Valley of Vision* (Banner of Truth, 2003), p 345.

things hold empire over the soul?"[47] That phrase, *where other things hold empire over the soul,* haunted me when I first read it. Likewise, the great theologian Augustine pleaded with the Lord: "Set love in order in me!"[48]

Your spiritual heart needs to get bigger to contain all that God has for you. Dreaming big is an invitation to hand over more of your life—more of your heart—to him. And we can dream big because God loves us.

- My friend Melissa knows God's love, and dreams of a time when all sex trafficking in the city is eradicated.

- My friend Morgan knows God's love, and dreams about shepherding God's people; he wants to make sure everyone is known and cared for and that no one falls through the cracks.

- My friend Joel knows God's love, and dreams of a time when hundreds of white, black, and brown people who don't know Jesus would come to our church and meet him.

They've tasted the love of God, and so they dream big dreams about more people experiencing that love for themselves. *Few of us are tempted today to dream too big*—but what if you had strength to know the height, length, depth, and breadth of the love of God?

---

47 Leonard Ravenhill, *Why Revival Tarries* (Baker Publishing Group, 2004), p 33.

48 Augustine, *City of God* XV.22.

BIG DREAMS

What does it look like to dream big for the glory of God? Paul continues in his letter to the Ephesians, "Now to him who is able"—that is, the God who spoke creation into existence, the God who parted the Red Sea, the God who raises the dead is able—"to do far more abundantly than all that we ask or think" (3:20).

Far more abundantly.

Some of your translations will say "immeasurably more" or "exceedingly abundantly." It's a double superlative. It's not good grammar; it's like saying "most bestest." But we're exhausted for words when trying to describe the ineffable, infinite, unimaginable power of God! One commentator wrote, "The Father's giving exceeds our capacity for asking or even dreaming."[49] We dream big because we have an abundance mindset. We have a God who is able to do abundantly more than all that we can pray or dream.

Do you have a scarcity mindset (an expectation that there won't be enough of what you need) or an abundance mindset (an expectation that there will)? Depending on your upbringing, you may lean one way or the other. But when we're talking about the kingdom of God, we should all have an abundance mindset. If you have a scarcity mindset about the kingdom of God, you have a theology problem—not a money or time or people problem. If we

---

49 Peter O'Brien, *Letter to the Ephesians: Pillar New Testament Commentary* (Eerdmans Publishing, 1999), p 266.

don't think that Jesus has an overabundance of whatever we might need in his back pocket, then our problem is that we don't really know God, not that we don't really know if we can do it.

Do you have a scarcity mindset? It's a disposition that I think we all seem to have to some degree. We operate in life from this place that says, *We don't have enough yet and we're not sure if we're going to get more, so we can't give.*

We don't have enough friends yet—we aren't in the inner circles, we haven't been accepted fully; we need more applause, more people liking us.

We need more money—we can't give, we can't be generous, because we don't have quite enough.

We need more time—we need space to do the things we want to do, so we must protect how we spend our days.

Until we realize that God is able to do "far more abundantly" than all that we can pray about or dream, we'll keep operating in the kingdom of this world. We'll develop a scarcity mindset that leads to anxiety and fear and exhaustion and apathy and impotence toward the kingdom of God.

We *can* risk our money by giving generously to what God is doing. We *can* risk our own reputation because God already delights in us.

Christians should be the most entrepreneurial, the most risk taking, the most audacious people in the world, because the Bible promises that God can do far more "than all that we ask or think." So we pray or dream or imagine something, and he'll do us one better!

> You want to plant other churches? Wait till you see what I'll do.
> You want to saturate your city with my glory and grace? I'll do even more than that.
> You want to see your neighborhoods transformed by the gospel? I'll do that and more.
> Ask me, church... Ask me to do something for my glory, and you'll see...

PRAYERFUL, FEARLESS, GENERATIONAL

Consider three ways for us to think about being a people that know God's love, know God's power, and dream big dreams for the kingdom of God.

1. OUR DREAMS NEED TO BE PRAYERFUL

God is able to do even more than we can *ask*. Your dreams might be too small if they don't scare you enough to pray. In *How to Pray*, Pete Greig says, "Our English word *prayer* derives from the Latin *precarius*. We pray because life is precarious."[50]

Praying might be your sole role in dreaming big for God's kingdom. You might not ever be the person who starts some new ministry or plants a church or leads a small

---

50 Pete Greig, *How to Pray: A Simple Guide for Normal People* (NavPress, 2019), p 4.

group or sells everything and moves to the Middle East, but if you pray huge prayers and lift up the people of God, the mighty hand of God will move—because he is able to do even more than you *ask*.

I've said this for years in my church, but one day in eternity, we'll find out that it was some sweet, quiet lady and her faithful prayers that Jesus will point to and say, *That's why I did all that work in you; I did what she asked and even more.*

If you dream big, you pray big.

2. OUR DREAMS NEED TO BE *FEARLESS*
Once again, in Ephesians 3:20, all of this is "according to the power at work within us." We can do it, *in him*.

We aren't afraid that we won't have the money or people or time or energy or favor or connections or authority—if we have an abundance mindset that says, *I'm a child of the richest and most powerful Dad in the universe.* He's got all we need, and then some. We are far too loved to need to be afraid to fail.

3. OUR DREAMS NEED TO BE *GENERATIONAL*
Paul says in verse 21 that this is true "throughout all generations." That means this promise is for us too. This promise to the 1st century church—that he's able to do even more than they ask or think, more than they can dream or imagine—is, in part, fulfilled in us! *We* are the promised generations!

Our dreams aren't big enough unless they leave a legacy. It's too small if our grandkids can't see it! Our dreams aren't big enough if they terminate with us. Our dreams aren't big enough unless they leave a gospel lineage.

- What do you dream God will do through you?

- What have you imagined?

- What might he be calling you to do that sounds crazy?

- Are you supposed to start a Bible study at work? Are you supposed to plant a church? Are you supposed to start a small group in your neighborhood? Are you supposed to give generously to underwrite kingdom advancement?

A CONCLUDING CAUTION

In 2023, from January 1st to about mid-March, we had a sort of mini-revival at our church. It was around the time of the outpouring of the Spirit at Asbury, but it started on the first Sunday of the year. We held just one service, since it was a holiday and many of our volunteers were out, and from the first note of the piano, there was a palpable sense of the Spirit in a uniquely profound way.

For three months, every Sunday seemed to have a little extra sweetness to it, and a little extra power. There were weeks of mighty stories where God was moving among us, with testimonies of healing, repentance, salvation, and prophecy. It culminated the Sunday before we moved into our permanent building, when we did something that probably no church should typically do! We held an open-mic Sunday, where our people could share the work of God in their lives over the past season, and the stories were filled with gospel greatness.

And then it was over.

Here's what I learned... I've prayed for revival for twelve years and got a small taste of it. I dreamed big, prayed huge, and God moved. And one of the main things I found is that *I wasn't quite ready for it.* My heart still needs to grow. My understanding of God's love is still weak. My character needs more work. I'm not holy enough for my bigger dreams yet. Other things still hold empire over my soul—there's still so much unconquered territory in my heart.

I've said it for years, but I think I understand it better now: God doesn't need me. He doesn't need my church. He doesn't need my tiny ideas, even if they seem like huge dreams to me. God doesn't need me to cover the earth with the knowledge of his glory like the waters flood the Atlantic. My ministry is merely a molecule of a drop of water in the ocean-deep glory of God—you can't even get your hands wet. Which means he's after something else.

He doesn't need *my* help; I need *his.*

So here's my concluding caution as you dream big (and do still dream big!): *God's dream for you is bigger than your dreams for him.* Surrender your dreams for his.

Remember, you are predestined to be conformed into the image of his Son (Romans 8:29). You *will* be like Jesus. So may the Spirit strengthen your heart with power. Would the Son rule on the throne of your whole heart. Would the Father's love be apprehended and comprehended by your inner being.

And, with your church, would you know all the fullness of God.

ACTION STEPS

- Do you pray for revival? Do you believe it's possible in your church context? Why not research one of the well-known revivals such as the Welsh revival of 1904.

- Consider what you pray for with regard to money, time, and relationships. Do you think you tend toward a scarcity or abundance mindset?

- How can you dream bigger dreams for God's glory? Write down Ephesians 3:20 as a reminder and speak it out loud to end your times of prayer this week.

CONCLUSION

God sends his church, and we love the church by *praying, giving, and going.*

Remember where we started? God's vision for the world is for his glory to saturate the whole earth—like water covers the sea. And God's vision for your life? An elect exile—chosen and precious, sent to a place not yet your home but knowing that you are loved by God.

Even now, I'm eager for you to read these words, believing that something is stirring in your heart toward the God who sends, and the church he's sent. Can you believe the God of the universe brings us along? It's like a cosmic go-to-work-with-Dad day. He doesn't need our help, but he wants it.

So, where do we go from here?

STARTING WITH PRAYER

The Moravians, who came from Bohemia in eastern Europe, started the modern mission movement led by German Reformer Count Zinzendorf. And it all began with prayer:

On August 13, 1727, they gathered for another ordinary church meeting. Zinzendorf preached a powerful sermon on the cross, and as he did, the Holy Spirit fell in such an overwhelming way that in that very moment, in that very meeting room, they began to confess their wrongs and forgive one another—no buts, no explanations, no holding back—just naming the wrongs and wiping the slate clean. The Spirit fell so heavily that they stayed for hours in confession… Two weeks after that night, they decided to start a prayer meeting. The prayer meeting lasted a hundred years.[51]

One hundred years of 24-7 prayer. In fact, they didn't send one missionary until they had seen five years of constant and consistent prayer.

"Hey, it's Dustin. I gotta tell you a story; call me back."

Dustin is a plumber. Likes beer. Hates texting. He's the only one in the world besides telemarketers who calls me on the phone. I called him back.

"I think I prayed a porn shop closed," he began.

For years, Dustin would drive past the store, and maybe shake his head in disapproval, not thinking much more about it. But one day, his spirit weighed heavy. He began to pray.

---

51 Tyler Staton, *Praying Like Monks, Living Like Fools* (Zondervan, 2022), p 85.

Dustin leads a small group in our church and shared his recent prayer efforts with them. Surprisingly, others in the group had also begun to pray that God would close it down. They committed to continual prayer, together now as a group, in unity that God's kingdom would come on earth as it is in heaven.

Dustin was driving home one day, and the shop's parking lot was empty. He cautiously(!) went through the parking lot to look closer and noticed a sign on the door. They were closing! A beer-drinking plumber (is there any other kind?) prayed a porn shop closed.

I thank my God in all my remembrance of you, always in every prayer of mine for you all making my prayer with joy, because of your partnership in the gospel from the first day until now. (Philippians 1:3-5)

The apostle Paul wrote from prison to a church he had planted in Philippi. Words were the only weapon he had. The pen was his sword; prayer was his power. Sent by the Spirit; shackled by Rome. But he sees the Philippian church as partners with him "in the gospel" (1:5)—literally the Greek word *koinonia* means they *share* with him in his mission. So he prays for them all the time, and it's safe to assume they have committed to pray for him too.

In our culture of hyper-activity, Protestant production, and poor work-life balance, prayer can seem passive. But perhaps it's the most powerful thing we do. Karl Barth said, "To clasp the hands in prayer is the beginning of an uprising against the disorder of the world."[52] Prayer is the best way to discern what God has for you next. Before you do anything else, prayer is the safest thing to do right now. Prayer in Jesus' name is the best way to exercise our authority in Christ. Prayer has the greatest chance to unite your will with God's. Pray!

Walter Wink writes the most audacious quote on prayer I've ever read:

> *No doubt, our intercessions sometimes change us as we open ourselves to new possibilities we had not guessed. No doubt, our prayers to God reflect back upon us as a divine command to become the answer to our prayer. But if we are to take the biblical understanding seriously, intercession is more than that.*
>
> *It changes the world and it changes what is possible. It creates an island of relative freedom in a world gripped by unholy necessity.*
> *A new force appears that hitherto was only potential. The entire configuration changes as the result of the change of a single part.*
> *A space opens in the praying person, permitting God to act without violating human freedom.*
>
> *History belongs to the intercessors, who believe the future into being.*

---

52 Quoted in Tyler Staton, *Praying Like Monks, Living Like Fools* (Zondervan, 2022), p 105-106.

If this is so, then intercession, far from being an escape from action, is a means of focusing for action and of creating action. By means of our intercessions we veritably cast fire upon the earth and trumpet the future into being.[53]

GIVING AND GOING

Prayer fueled the Moravian mission effort; but God often answers the prayers of his people *with* his people.

We pray for his kingdom to come, and he sometimes answers by calling us to go.

We pray for his glory to be known, and he sometimes answers by sending us to where it's not known.

We pray that he would provide for the advancement of his kingdom, and he sometimes answers by calling us to radical generosity.

Have you ever thought about this? *You* might be God's answer to someone's prayers.

Each family in Zinzendorf's church would partner with a missionary sent out in prayer and financial support. Intercession and mission, senders and goers, working together to extraordinary effect.[54] In less than 30 years, before Zinzendorf's death, they sent 226 missionaries from their small community into 10 nations. The

---

53 Walter Wink, *Engaging the Powers* (Fortress, 2017), p 322.

54 Pete Greig, *How to Pray: A Simple Guide for Normal People* (NavPress, 2019), p 111.

Moravians were so committed to missions that 29 of them sold themselves into slavery to reach the slaves on the island of St. Thomas. Twenty-two of them died.

Of course, God is honored in our ordinary lives as we seek to live unto his glory in the mundane work of laundry and school and dishes and kids' sports. But our sent-ness infuses intentionality in all that we do. Every dollar we have is a kingdom dollar. Every minute we live is a kingdom minute. Every place we go, the kingdom will one day reign like the waters cover the seas.

So, as you pray, just know that God may answer your prayers by calling you to give or give more. He may call you to go, or to live more on mission where you are. The very message of the gospel is that Jesus was sent first to you. That God *gave* his only Son for us. "As the Father has sent me, even so I am sending you" (John 20:21).

The church is sent. We are in the midst of a global movement that is advancing in every culture and place. God's kingdom is coming, for his King has triumphed, and he has chosen his Bride. The people of God are invited into the mission of God for the glory of God.

This is what you are a part of! God has a vision for the world, and he's inviting you in. So will you pray, give, or go?

Send

ACKNOWLEDGMENTS

I wrote this book while moving our church into a permanent building, getting hit by a car (true story), and preaching through the book of Revelation. That was only possible because of the community of faith and love around me as well as a great team.

I'm so grateful for my assistant, Sarah Metcalfe, in all things. Nothing happens without her.

I was supported and motivated by my friend and best-selling author, Derrick Kinney, who cheered me on (and bribed/rewarded me with wine and good food) after each chapter was written.

Carl Laferton and the team at The Good Book Company were outstanding to work with. Catherine Durant made literally every paragraph better and I can't imagine the book without her.

I'm so grateful to shepherd a people like The Paradox Church who live their lives sent for the sake of the gospel. They love the Bible, Jesus, and his mission; it's such a joy to serve them.

Thank you Ryan, Jake, Kaynenn, Brad, Matt, Caleb, Ben K, Ben C, Joel, Melissa, and many more for your partnership in Fort Worth to mobilize God's people on mission.

And, finally, thank you to my family: Heather, Harper, Hollis, and Hadden, for putting up with my late nights, busy mind, and (sometimes) cranky mornings. God has primarily sent me to you, and you to me, and I love you dearly.

DISCUSSION GUIDE FOR SMALL GROUPS

1. GOD'S VISION FOR THE WORLD

1. Read Habakkuk 1:1-4, 12-13. What catches your eye in these verses? In what ways do Habakkuk's complaints still ring true today?

2. How do the ideas in these verses affect our sense of hope and expectation about what God can do? How have they affected you personally?

3. Read Habakkuk 2:14. What do you think it means for the earth to be "filled with the knowledge of the glory of the LORD"? (You may like to have a look at page 18 and consider the questions in the third paragraph.)

4. Do you have a vision for seeing God's glory come to a particular community, place, or area of life? What are you longing for specifically?

5. What do you think it looks like to live by faith in regard to that thing? (See pages 21-22 for more on this.)

6. What is the role of the local church in all of this? How could you pray for your church in light of what you've read?

2. GOD'S VISION FOR US

1. Have you ever felt like an "exile" or misfit because of your faith? What happened?

2. Read Acts 9:31. How did God use the physical exile and scatteredness of his people to build up the church? (Re-read pages 30-31 for more help on this.) How can this encourage us when we feel out of place today?

3. What do you think it means to walk in the fear of the Lord? When we do this, how might it change our view of what happens to us in our lives?

4. Read the verses about the work of the Holy Spirit, listed on page 36. Do any of these surprise you or jump out at you? Which do you most need to hear today?

5. Think of a time when you clearly saw God at work in your church or community, or in yourself or another individual. What role do you think the fear of the Lord and the comfort of the Spirit played?

6. How do you feel about the idea of being part of a church that multiplies? Does this challenge you, excite you, worry you? Pray for one another in the light of what you've discussed.

3. CHURCH PLANTING

1. Consider your preconceptions about church planting. If someone asked you to be part of a church-planting team, what would your instinctive reaction be and why?

2. Read Matthew 28:18-20 and Acts 14:21-23. What did Paul and Barnabas ("they" in the Acts passage) do in order to carry out Jesus' instructions? Why do you think it was important to appoint church leaders (elders) and organize the new Christians into churches?

3. "Planting new churches is the best way to reach new cultures" (page 49). If you're in an established church, consider what kinds of people you tend to reach with the gospel, and what kinds of people you're not reaching. Are there "new cultures" that you aren't connecting with?

4. What could it look like to have more of a "sending culture" in your church generally? (Look back at "Anchor #1" on page 52 to prompt thoughts on this.)

5. How can we cultivate an abundance mindset and avoid a scarcity mindset? (Look back at "Anchor #3" on page 54 for help.)

6. What do you think about church planting as a result of reading this chapter? What leaps out at you as a great reason to plant, or a great comfort and motivator?

4. THE GLOBAL GOD

1. Read Acts 8:1-8. How do you think you would have felt during the events of verse 1? How would your perspective have changed after that?

2. Why do you think it is so important to remember that the church has a global mission? What is the result when we forget?

3. The heading on page 68 reads "Senders: Pray. Care. Fund." Praying and funding are probably very familiar concepts when we think about sending missionaries. But what about caring for those we send, even after they've gone? What do you think it looks like to do this well?

4. Re-read pages 70-71. What are you most encouraged and most challenged by here?

5. Read Revelation 5:6-14. Take some time to pause over the words here. What makes Jesus (the Lamb) so worthy? How can you praise and pray in the light of this passage?

6. Do you have missionaries connected with your church? What could you do to encourage and support them this week?

5. A REDEMPTIVE PRESENCE

1. Take some time to discuss the place or places where you live. How would you describe it and the people who live there? What is specific or special about this community? What is difficult or a problem there?

2. Re-read the section "Right Hand, Left Hand" (pages 76-78). How do you respond to this metaphor of two hands working together? How is your church doing at employing both "hands"?

3. How could you pray for the area where you live—for its flourishing? Identify a few key areas of need and spend some time in prayer now.

4. How does your faith in the gospel affect the way you do your work (including unpaid work)? In what ways is God using your work to contribute to the flourishing of you and others? (Re-read the quotation from Timothy Keller on pages 81-82 if you get stuck.)

5. How do you feel about getting involved in working for justice in your city? If you are already doing this, how have you seen the Lord at work? If you are not, what could you consider trying?

6. Read Acts 17:26-27. This passage shows us that wherever we are is where God has sent us. Spend some time worshiping God for his good plans and surrendering yourselves to his work in your local area.

6. FINDING YOUR PLACE

1. Think about your life so far. In what ways have you seen God's providence at work—his plan working itself out through the seemingly unforeseen circumstances of your life? In particular, how has he enabled you to serve and love others?

2. Read 1 Corinthians 12:4-11 and Romans 12:4-8. What gifts are mentioned here? Can you think of an example of each one?

3. In pairs, work through the questions in the section "Discerning Your Gift."

4. What has God already called you to? (It might be your family, or a specific ministry within your church or community, or something else.) How would you describe that call? How do you think you are doing at responding to it?

5. If someone came to you and said that they felt called to something, how would you respond? Use the questions on pages 99-100 to come up with your ideal response.

6. Is there anything you need to go away and think about, or do, in response to what you've read in this chapter? Pray for one another now as you consider God's call on your lives.

7. GOSPEL GOODBYES

1. Read Acts 20:17-38. What was the relationship like between Paul and the elders at Ephesus? What was good about this? What was hard about this?

2. When a small group splits or members of a church leave to plant a new congregation, what might be difficult about that—both for those leaving and for those being left behind?

3. Look at the advice Paul gives to the Ephesian elders in Acts 20:28-32. How could these words both warn and encourage those who face the uncomfortableness of going or sending?

4. Why is it helpful to allow ourselves to grieve the losses we feel when someone leaves, or when we leave, a community? If there are losses you have felt personally, you might like to share them and grieve together now.

5. Has anyone been sent out from your church or small group? What small steps can you take this week to encourage and support them, even though you're not together anymore?

6. This concept of gospel goodbyes is a challenge to our desire for security and stability. What do you find hard or confronting about this idea? What comforts can you find in the chapter you've read? (Look particularly at pages 108-109 for help with this.)

8. DREAM BIG & CONCLUSION

1. What do you think of when you hear the word "revival"? Are there any ways in which this chapter has altered your thinking about that word?

2. Read Ephesians 3:14-21 slowly. What is Paul praying for here? What is "big" about his prayer?

3. How would you pray this for yourself? In what ways do you long to know the love of Christ more, be more filled with him, or anything else Paul mentions?

4. How would you pray this for your city or your church?

5. What do you think people in your church fear risking? Money, time, relationships? What would it look like in your church to have more of a culture of giving, and of assuming that the Lord will do more than you ask or imagine?

6. What is one thing that has struck you in this book that you want to take away and keep with you? How do you hope that God will change you, your church, and your community as a result of reading this book?

7. Spend time in prayer together. You might like to start with some prayers based on Ephesians 3:14-21. Lift up one another to Christ and ask for his Spirit to work powerfully and abundantly in you. After you have prayed more generally, you may like to share specific requests about individuals or communities to whom you feel God is sending you or others you know.

LOVE YOUR CHURCH

loveyourchurchseries.com

the good book

COMPANY

BIBLICAL | RELEVANT | ACCESSIBLE

At The Good Book Company, we are dedicated to helping Christians and local churches grow. We believe that God's growth process always starts with hearing clearly what he has said to us through his timeless word—the Bible.

Ever since we opened our doors in 1991, we have been striving to produce Bible-based resources that bring glory to God. We have grown to become an international provider of user-friendly resources to the Christian community, with believers of all backgrounds and denominations using our books, Bible studies, devotionals, evangelistic resources, and DVD-based courses.

We want to equip ordinary Christians to live for Christ day by day, and churches to grow in their knowledge of God, their love for one another, and the effectiveness of their outreach.

Call us for a discussion of your needs or visit one of our local websites for more information on the resources and services we provide.

Your friends at The Good Book Company

thegoodbook.com | thegoodbook.co.uk
thegoodbook.com.au | thegoodbook.co.nz
thegoodbook.co.in